Early Voices
of
Conscious
Evolution

Early Voices
of
Conscious
Evolution

Insight and Inspiration from the
Beginning of the Modern Era

Edited by

Matthew Shapiro

Plusvalent Press

Boise

Plusvalent Press

ISBN 979-8-9896403-0-0 (paperback)

ISBN 979-8-9896403-1-7 (electronic)

Library of Congress Control Number: 2023923568

Printed in the United States of America

*This work is dedicated to the late
Jonas Salk
and
Bela H. Banathy,
and to Alexander Christakis,
who all offered validation and
encouragement to a young upstart,
and to
Mary Parker Follett (1868-1933),
who supplied my first clue that the
idea of conscious evolution existed
more than a century ago.*

Contents

Introduction

It seems that the dominant characteristic of our day is change. Change and tension. The tension, I suggest, comes from the situation that while we know that we *could* address the great problems that we face, we, ourselves, stand in the way of doing it. This tension gets to the theme of the following anthology, because this tension is not new. It actually began to emerge around the middle of the 19th century. In fact, we can mark that time as the beginning of an era distinctly different from that of the previous 12,000 years or so of human history, dating to the beginnings of stable societies and cultures. It can even be said that this new era finds its place in an evolutionary story that can be traced to the formation of the earth, and to the formation of the universe before it. This collection is meant to serve as evidence— testimony might be a better word—of an awareness of this transition.

The anthology consists of excerpts of writings from the Industrial and Progressive Eras. I chose the passages that appear herein because I felt that they demonstrate or exemplify an awareness on the part of the authors that a fundamental shift was occurring in the world—a growing out of the relatively unconscious evolution of society and culture that characterized nearly all of human history, and toward *conscious evolution*. By conscious evolution I mean a new capacity for people, on a global scale, to reflect on their society and culture and to realize that these could be intentionally evolved, through cooperative effort, toward forms that were better for people, for all of the institutions of people, and for the entire planet.

There would have been several catalysts for this shift. One was the Industrial Revolution, which included revolutions in communication on a global scale; revolutions in transportation that brought nations, continents, and cultures into much more intimate contact; and dramatic accelerations in population growth, urban growth, and economic shifts toward industrialization. These forces spurred a tremendous growth in material wealth, along with great gaps in wealth and living conditions and perceptions of injustice that gave rise to a range of social change movements. Paralleling and interacting with these came a range of new sciences, including psychology, sociology, and anthropology, which turned a mirror toward human nature and the human condition.

The second major catalyst for this shift was Darwin's new theory of evolution (among other competing theories about change in species). It was not long before thinkers like Herbert Spencer began to apply the concept of evolution far beyond the arena of biology, tracing its forms from the beginning of the cosmos all the way up through social phenomena of their age. (Some traced the earliest roots of evolutionary thinking in the social arena to pre-Darwinian thinkers like Kant and Hegel, among others.)

Recognition of the conscious changeability of society also built, of course, upon some of the innovations of recent prior generations—the Scientific Revolution and representative forms of government in particular. However, these developments in and of themselves could not yet create or enable the broad reflectiveness that was needed for evolutionary awareness and the concept of conscious evolution. That required the combination of a popular theory of evolution and the catalyst of an Industrial Revolution.

Why Assemble This Collection?

For many years now, I've used the framework of *general evolution theory* to understand the direction of change across the history of the universe and of life on earth, through the present day—not out of a purely academic interest, but because it put a context to the kind of advocacy and activism work that I've always been drawn to. Over the years, it became apparent to me that the mid-19th century was the time when the most recent shift between major evolutionary eras was beginning. I was aware, as are most with an interest in history, of the general renaissance of thinking that occurred during the Industrial Era and into what is known as the Progressive Era. But I felt a need to look for specific evidence that underlying this shift in thinking, and associated changes in society, was dramatic growth in evolutionary awareness and a recognition of the capacity for conscious evolution. That is why I decided to seek out voices from the time.

Why is it helpful to look back at this time, to read this "testimony"? It is not merely for intellectual exercise. It is meant to provide *context* to our times, and context is key to *meaning*. Meaning, in turn, can help inform, even inspire. Recognizing this chapter of evolutionary history fosters evolutionary *awareness* in the present generation; evolutionary awareness lays the groundwork for evolutionary *consciousness*, and evolutionary consciousness invites evolutionary *action*.

There is much good work going on in the world—work mostly related to the emancipation of people combined with the integration of people to create better for all. This kind of work— what we may call "socially progressive" (and later inclusive of environmental advocacy and activism)—really began more than 150 years ago. Understanding the larger evolutionary context in which that work began, and in which it is happening today, opens up the possibility for reflection that can help make that work more effective and inclusive. But it also opens up the potential for a different and arguably more powerful kind of work for positive change—work that is focused not on specific problems and issues but on building the capacity among people to see deeper, work deeper, and to work at the level of patterns that give rise to those problems in the first place. This, ultimately, was my motivation for curating this collection.

It is my hope that the reader will find gems in the individual passages as well as glean a sense of the changing winds from the works taken as a whole. It is my further hope that the reader will, from this collection, increase their own evolutionary awareness and help empower their own part in the conscious co-evolution of society, individual, and nature.

Criteria for Selection

In creating this anthology, I looked for passages that provided evidence of the following, particularly if they were explicitly connected to the theme of evolution or to the emergence of human agency and a rising consciousness across societies or across the planet:

- knowledge that a significant shift had taken place in social consciousness, specifically the emergence of agency regarding the direction and shape of society
- recognition that biology was no longer "center stage" in evolution
- recognition that the unprecedented rate of change in society, industrialization and responses to it, and the theory of evolution were driving the aforementioned shift in consciousness
- observation of the fundamental differences between contemporary social and cultural awareness and that awareness characterizing prior human history
- a recognition of the power of ideas and the importance of idealism and vision
- recognition of the emergence of new (social) sciences as a mirror to society

- a view that the individual evolves in their own lifetime, and that society and individual can and should *co*-evolve, rising together
- democracy as a characteristic of the evolutionary shift, particularly democracy as a participatory and creative process
- concerns about justice, ethics, and the less privileged
- advocacy for inclusiveness, such as a recognition of gender, racial, ethnic, and other social biases in society and articulation of why inclusion of the excluded benefits all
- reference to planetary or global interdependence, and to the emergence of a new kind of awareness or consciousness, for the first time on a planetary or civilization level
- recognition that society can and should be improved, that it is a work-in-progress, and that the journey toward greater progress would likely have no end
- placement of the shift in human consciousness within the widest context of cosmic evolution
- recognition of the dramatic effects of technology on society and the risk of cultural wisdom lagging behind technology
- evidence of a systems perspective, including recognition of rising complexity and interrelatedness among issues and dimensions of society, and across the planet
- recognition of the role of institutions, particularly education, in fostering a greater sense of agency, along with critiques of institutions not keeping pace with the needs of individuals and society
- recognition that peace—as a constructive relationship— could and should transcend war

- ecological or environmental awareness, specifically in response to the harm that industrialization could bring

The above set of criteria clearly casts a wide net, and it should be obvious that I did not include everything that could have been included. I did not attempt to be encyclopedic in my search or my curation of the anthology. However, I believe that the selection of passages serves as an effective body of evidence.

Observations about the Authors and their Ideas

The authors cited herein are not a homogeneous group. They lived and worked across a period of many decades, had different backgrounds and careers, philosophies and religious beliefs, associations, statures and genders. Some were biologists by training, some sociologists, historians, and anthropologists, others social workers, ministers, psychologists, educators, or poets. Some were well-known, others less so. Their interpretations of evolution varied. Most of the authors were men, and all but two, to my knowledge, were Anglo-Saxon/white. Many authors apparently identified as Christian. Many were also ecumenical or even anti-theological, such as the humanists who formed the ethical culture movement of the turn of the 20th century.

Most authors seemed to hold the prevailing views on race at the time, including the idea of inherent superiorities and inferiorities. Many also wrote in terms that we would today recognize as imperialistic and Western-centric, speaking of so-called civilized and savage races or peoples. Some still saw biology as a part of the path of continuing evolutionary improvement, via eugenics—a term that authors used variously to mean anything from controlled reproduction to good motherhood. None of the quoted authors appeared to see biological control as a primary strategy, however, and some explicitly said that the path forward was strictly one of cultural and social evolution. Many spoke in terms of "the race" as the entirety of humanity, and all or most seemed to emphasize the need for social changes that would benefit all people. Some expressed a "cosmopolitan" view, and some appeared to see an equality of advancement between east and west.

Many of the authors used the words *moral* and *ethical* or *ethics*, these being considered integral to a shift into conscious evolution. Some proclaimed that Christianity would play a key role in the positive evolution of society, but such authors reconciled their faith with evolutionary theory, in some cases seeing the evolutionary process as a divine cosmic process, and focusing on an ethical rather than otherworldly mission. A significant number of the authors speaking from a faith perspective were from the Unitarian Universalist tradition.

Many of the authors spoke of rationality and the emergence of a rational society. Science was held in very high regard as a guiding star in social progress. This was primarily seen through the application of social sciences, all of which were relatively new, rather than via the technological products of society. Some of the authors could be associated with the school of modernist technocratic management that was one of the streams of the Progressive Era. Many seemed to emphasize more organic philosophies. Technology was spoken of as a catalyst of change and something that culture and society needed to learn how to manage better so that it would serve, rather than endanger, humankind and quality of life.

Many authors placed great faith in the new institution of public education, some even equating education with conscious evolution. In fact, education was probably the most highly cited means to a better society. However, some expressed concern about the direction being taken by institutionalized education, noting how it was already failing to keep pace with the needs of society.

Some authors—particularly those whose writings date to the late 1800s and turn of the 20th century—saw hope in the new idea of socialism as an obvious next step in societal evolution. This was, of course, well before the Russian Revolution. Others were skeptical that socialism was the only or the best path forward.

In terms of the unfolding of evolutionary theory, Herbert Spencer was generally acknowledged as pioneer of evolutionary thought as it might apply to society. However, most of the authors reviewed seemed to reject the idea of "Social Darwinism" that Spencer is known for. Several noted how cooperation was as much, or even more, a feature of evolution than competition, challenging the simplistic notion of "survival of the fittest" and its implication of competition. While some placed the new stage of evolution in the context of the broadest pattern of cosmic evolution, most did not see the new evolution as a continuation of previous "organic" processes of evolution. They instead saw changes in social policy and institutions toward social betterment as being based on consciousness and choice. Some were *co-evolutionary* in the sense of focusing on the mutual interdependence of evolution at the individual and societal levels.

Where the term *utopian* was used, it was done so not in the caricatured fashion of seeking an impossibly perfect place, but rather in terms of a journey. Many expressed the view that evolution would be a never-ending process, as perfection was to be found in an ever-adjusting direction, not in an achievable destination.

What we would today refer to as environmental sustainability or stewardship was not a prominent theme encountered, although some authors did speak directly to it. That said, it should be noted that conservation movements and institutions were indeed starting to emerge throughout this time period.

The writings that I surveyed also suggest a conscious recognition of the tension or conflict at the time between a number of core philosophical, cultural, or social values and worldviews. Examples of ostensibly opposing tendencies noted in some of these writings included:

- individual vs. collective
- natural/organic vs. artificial/mechanical
- realism vs. idealism
- conservatism vs. progressivism
- altruism vs. egoism
- nationalism vs. cosmopolitanism
- science vs. spirituality

More noteworthy was the recognition of the need for an integration or reconciliation of these seemingly opposing principles and forces.

The earlier writings in particular evidenced tremendous optimism and faith in progress. This optimism continues throughout the collection, but some authors tempered this optimism with concerns or admonition about the importance of going forward "eyes wide open." The First World War dealt a blow to the previous faith in an impending golden age, appearing to serve as a reality check. Based on most of the post-war passages, the war seemed to be a fresh impetus for conscious evolutionary thought in the 1920s and 30s.

In closing, I thought it worth mentioning some notable gatherings that took place during the era. The World's Columbian Exposition (Chicago World's Fair) of 1893 included the World's Congress of Representative Women, the World's Parliament of Religions, and the fifth Universal Peace Congress, and the First Universal Races Congress of 1911 (London) was centered around anti-racism. These gatherings were signs of changing times, if not of transformation.

Admissions, Disclaimers, and Caveats

The inclusion of this set of passages from this set of particular authors was based purely on my view of their strength as evidence of thought patterns associated with the idea or process of conscious evolution. Their inclusion is not an indication of my subscribing to those authors or their views, and I make no representation as to the quality of their theories or viewpoints. This is particularly true of allusions to racial or cultural superiority and to the advocacy for eugenics that characterized some of the thinkers of the time.

I would also add that the selections were drawn from the limited body of seemingly relevant works that I was able to find or stumble upon. The body of selections is therefore not encyclopedic, nor was it intended to be. I make no claim of comprehensiveness.

I will also acknowledge that selection and editing of these passages was imperfect and unavoidably reflects my biases, conscious or unconscious. I tried to capture the representative, the essential, the powerful, and the unique. While I hoped to capture a wide range of perspectives and themes within the overall theme, and was rewarded in the search by encountering a good variety, I make no claim of balance to the selections.

Related to range of perspectives, and to diversity, the vast majority of published voices found in my research from this time period were those of white males from either the United States or the UK. While this finding is primarily a reflection of the times, it is certain that people other than published white folk of the Western world also had insights into the emerging streams of conscious evolution, and I acknowledge that additional effort may have yielded additional, more diverse voices and passages worthy of inclusion in this collection.

A Word About Editing & Formatting

The passages selected are presented in chronological order of their original publication date. In incorporating the selected passages, I tried to minimize editing. Spelling was left as in the original, and any italicization within the selections is from the original. Where, for the sake of conciseness, I removed words within sentences, or needed to bridge sentences within paragraphs with some words or sentences between them omitted, I inserted ellipses. Brackets ([ ]) of course indicate where I substituted a capital letter for an original lower-case letter, or where I inserted a word for clarity.

Where I drew more than one distinct passage from a particular source, I inserted a series of dots to separate the quotations:

. . . . . .

I used a larger, bolder series of dots to separate selections from completely different sources:

● ● ● ● ● ●

The author, source, and year are given at the beginning of each selection. Full citations are in the *Sources* section. I have not included page numbers in the citations, for the sake of avoiding an academic style to the work.

Topic-Author Index

<u>Notes on the Index:</u>

- The passages indexed to each topic were selected based on their having the most direct association with the topics as observed by the editor. Indexing is not exhaustive or perfect, and there can be a subtle interweaving of a wider range of subjects in many of the passages.
- The original sources for the selections may relate to a wider range of subjects than is reflected in the narrower passages chosen for the anthology.
- Authors are listed in chronological order of appearance in the anthology.

complexity, increase in, challenge in addressing	Brosius 1895; Jones 1899; Howerth 1908; Bobbitt 1918; Bernard 1922; Marvin 1923; Beck 1926; Mukerjee 1932
conscious evolution, evolutionary agency	Cairnes 1875; Clapperton 1885; Powell 1885; Sence 1888; Seth 1889; Le Conte 1891; Perry-Coste 1894; Dyer 1895; James 1895; Leppington 1895; Hobhouse 1901; Howerth 1902; Hird 1903; Ashcroft 1905; Untermann 1905; Davidson 1907; Sprague 1909; Robinson 1912; Kimball 1913; Wallas 1914; Vestal 1917; Kracht 1917; Follett 1918; Branford 1919; Partridge 1919; Conklin 1919; de Bothezat 1919; Swift 1919; McCabe 1920; Patten 1920; The Arbitrator 1920; Cohen 1921; Loy 1921; Ogburn 1922; Seashore 1922; Bernard 1923; Wissler 1923; Darsie 1924; Hart 1924; Bennett 1925; Catt 1925; Ellwood 1925; Kelloway 1925; Ellwood 1927; Millikan 1928; McCabe 1932; Samuel 1935; Churchill 1937; Cameron 1938; Huxley 1959
conservative and progressive, role for both	Spiller 1916; Ellwood 1925
cooperation, social interdependence	Wilkin 1903; Untermann 1905; Howerth 1908; Bushnell 1913; Kimball 1913; Spiller 1916; Meredith 1916; Follett 1918; Conklin 1919; Marvin

1923; Herrick 1924; Boodin 1925; Noble 1926; Ellwood 1927; Mukerjee 1932

cosmic or universal evolution, context of

Spencer 1874; Janes 1895; Kidd 1902; Hird 1903; Wilkin 1903; Untermann 1905; Quarterly 1907; Greenlaw 1917; Follett 1918; McCabe 1920; Teilhard de Chardin 1920; Weiss 1923; Macdonald 1924; Kelloway 1925; Noble 1926; Hertzler 1928; Mukerjee 1932; Samuel 1935; Huxley 1959

culture, existence or role of

Ogburn 1922; Wissler 1923; Faris 1926; Ellwood 1927; Moreno 1934

democracy

Dewey 1903; Howerth 1908; Bushnell 1913; Weyl 1914; Meredith 1916; Greenlaw 1917; Vestal 1917; Follett 1918; Bobbitt 1918; Kilpatrick 1921; Loy 1921; Newton 1922

ecological impact, awareness

Marsh 1874; Howerth 1908; Gray 1913; Kimball 1913; Geddes 1917; Patten 1920; Yard 1923; Herrick 1924; Mukerjee 1932

economics, sustainable

Gray 1913; Mukerjee 1925; Mukerjee 1932

education, importance of; and society

Ellis 1866; Savage 1889; Dyer 1895; Dabney 1896; Reclus 1896; Dewey 1903; Davidson 1907; Quarterly 1907; Welch 1910; Robinson 1912; Spiller 1916; Bobbitt 1918; Kilpatrick 1921;

Bernard 1922; Hart 1924; Kilpatrick 1926; Ellwood 1927; Millikan 1928

entropy, reversal of   Herrick 1924

equity, equality, inclusiveness   Harrison 1882; Reclus 1896; Maeterlinck 1907; Cooley 1909; Conn 1914; Taft 1915; Tuttle 1915; Meredith 1916; Pickens 1916; Spiller 1916; Thomson 1924

ethics, morality, role in conscious society; evolutionary ethic, responsibility   Powell 1887; Savage 1889; Janes 1895; Dyer 1895; Jones 1899; Bixby 1907; Sprague 1909; Conn 1914; Geddes 1917; Greenlaw 1917; Kracht 1917; Conklin 1919; de Bothezat 1919; Kilpatrick 1926; Samuel 1935

evolution, theory or story of, significance of   Powell 1887; Savage 1889; Catt 1893; Kimball 1913; McCabe 1920; Patten 1920; Marvin 1923; Hart 1924; Catt 1925; Millikan 1928; Huxley 1959

evolution, process or dynamic of   Spencer 1874; Perry-Coste 1894; Brosius 1895; Dyer 1895; Hobhouse 1901; Kimball 1913; Conn 1914; Branford 1919; Kelloway 1925; Ellwood 1925; Mukerjee 1932; Whitehead 1933

evolution, purposeful, telos or ends   Reade 1872; Dyer 1895; Howerth 1902; Patten 1920; Kelloway 1925; Mukerjee 1925; Mukerjee 1932

ideals, idealism, role and importance of	Le Conte 1891; Dyer 1895; Reclus 1896; Maeterlinck 1907; Howerth 1908; Sprague 1909; Welch 1910; Geddes 1915; Spiller 1916; McGilvary 1916; Kracht 1917; Geddes 1917; McCabe 1920; Kilpatrick 1921; Loy 1921; Mecklin 1922; Newton 1922; Darsie 1924; Sarton 1924; Ellwood 1925; Mukerjee 1925; Whitehead 1925; Whitehead 1933
individual, the; importance of, effect, relation to society	Montague 1885; Spence 1888; Savage 1889; Perry-Coste 1894; Small & Vincent 1894; Brosius 1895; Dyer 1895; Jones 1898; Wilkin 1903; Conn 1914; Kracht 1917; Follett 1918; Darsie 1924; Boodin 1925; Kelloway 1925; Hertzler 1928; Samuel 1935; Huxley 1959
individual, support for development of	Strong 1893; Dyer 1895; Dabney 1896; Jones 1898; Wilkin 1903; Goode 1904; Tayler 1906; Wilshire 1906; Sprague 1909; Staars 1909; Swift 1912; Conn 1914; Tuttle 1915; Meredith 1916; Geddes 1917; Weiss 1923; Thomson 1924; Kilpatrick 1926
industrialization, response to problems caused by; mechanization of life	Harrison 1882; Dyer 1895; Bushnell 1913; Vestal 1917; Geddes 1917; Mecklin 1922; Ogburn 1922; Thomson 1924; Beck 1926; Kilpatrick 1926; Moreno 1934

planetary or global scale	Reclus 1896; Wilkin 1903; Bushnell 1913; Kimball 1913; Wallas 1914; Richard 1914; Spiller 1916; Prince 1916; Greenlaw 1917; Follett 1918; Bobbitt 1918; Branford 1919; Patten 1920; Teilhard de Chardin, 1920; Kilpatrick 1921; Wells 1921; Seashore 1922; Rust 1923; Sarton 1924; Boodin 1925; Hertzler 1928
popular desire, discontent; masses	Strong 1893; Davis 1908; Bobbitt 1918
rational, rationalism, rationalization, use of reason and intelligence	Le Conte 1891; Wilkin 1903; Howerth 1908; Cooley 1909; Pickens 1916; Greenlaw 1917; Follett 1918; Conklin 1919; Cohen 1921; Kilpatrick 1921; Loy 1921; Bernard 1923; Wissler 1923; Herrick 1924; Ellwood 1927
science, faith in	Reade 1872; Clapperton 1885; Spiller 1916; Geddes 1917; Cohen 1921; Newton 1922; Marvin 1923; Ellwood 1925; Ellwood 1927; Millikan 1928; Samuel 1935
social conditions, social improvement, progress in; evidence of or lack of progress	Ellis 1866; Reade 1872; Harrison 1882; Catt 1893; Strong 1893; Small & Vincent 1894; Reclus 1896; Jones 1899; Kidd 1902; Howerth 1902; Quarterly 1907; Maeterlinck 1907; Davis 1908; Sprague 1909; Wallas 1914; Weyl 1914; Meredith 1914; Kracht 1917; Follett 1918; Ogburn 1922; Seashore 1922;

Marvin 1923; Thomson 1924; Kelloway 1925; Faris 1926

social consciousness   The Spectator & Lowell 1884; Perry-Coste 1894; Small & Vincent 1894; Brosius 1895; Reclus 1896; Howerth 1902; Davis 1908; Cooley 1909; Bushnell 1913; Taft 1915; Prince 1916; Kracht 1917; Follett 1918; Patten 1920; Loy 1921; Hertzler 1928

social evolution, era of, as distinct from biological evolution; social evolution taking center-stage   Le Conte, 1891; Dyer 1895; Reid 1897; Conn 1914; Spiller 1916; Kracht 1917; Follett 1918; Conklin 1919; Teilhard de Chardin 1920; Cohen 1921; Conklin 1921; Weiss 1923; Marvin 1923; Kelloway 1925; Ellwood 1927; Millikan 1928

social influences, taking precedence over natural   Le Conte, 1891; Goode 1904; Kimball 1913; Conn 1914; Follett 1918; Bernard 1922; Ogburn 1922; Seashore 1922; Thomson 1924

social invention, vs. mechanical, lag between   Ogburn 1922; Bernard 1923; Kilpatrick 1926; Ogburn & Gilfillan 1933

social sciences, new; sociology   Tylor 1873; Wilkin 1903; Robinson 1912; Bernard 1922; Bernard 1923; Wissler 1923; Faris 1926; Ellwood 1927; Ogburn 1933; Kamiat 1934

society, conscious	Montague 1885; Small & Vincent 1894; Howerth 1902; Ely 1903; Wilkin 1903; Bernard 1923; Wissler 1923
specialization of knowledge, problems with	Wallas 1914; Beck 1926; Kamiat 1934; Huxley 1959
spiritual aspect, religion	Reade 1872; Clapperton 1885; Savage 1889; Wilshire 1906; Bushnell 1913; Greenlaw 1917; Follett 1918; Branford 1919; Newton 1922; Sarton 1924; Ellwood 1927; Mukerjee 1932; Samuel 1935
technology & material invention, effects of; outpacing cultural maturity	Ellis 1866; Harrison 1882; Powell 1887; Strong 1893; Dyer 1895; Reclus 1896; Kimball 1913; Wallas 1914; Richard, 1914; Tuttle 1915; Geddes 1917; de Bothezat 1919; Patten 1920; Kilpatrick 1921; Van Loon 1921; Wells 1921; Ogburn 1922; Mecklin 1922; Rust 1923; Boodin 1924; Beck 1926; Kilpatrick 1926; Burroughs 1927; Millikan 1928; Wells 1928/1933; Moreno 1934; Churchill 1937; Van Loon 1938
transformative approaches, in contrast with treating symptoms	Sprague 1909; Follett 1918; The Arbitrator 1920; Cohen 1921

Passages

William Ellis
Thoughts on the Future of The Human Race (1866)

With the progress of time, men have had opportunities for observing how far the occurrences of each successive day and year and century have corresponded or conflicted with their previous expectations; and they have found themselves confirmed in some of their expectations, and mistaken in others, but growing in capacity of correct prognostication...Combined with this greater ability of foretelling the future, has also been a greater ability of bringing about one kind of future rather than another, and a clearer appreciation of the kind of future which it is desirable to bring about.

. . . . . .

A survey of some of the causes or forces actually at work through human beings will prepare us to judge how far they have shifted or altered from causes or forces heretofore at work, and hence how far altered effects or results are to be looked for. Among these causes or forces may be cited—

1. The wider range of man's knowledge and his greater aptitude in applying it, both in the production of wealth for the purpose of increasing well-being.
2. A more accurate appreciation of the method by which attainments in knowledge and skill may be imparted from one generation to its successors, with the character and disposition to induce that conduct in individuals which is likely to promote, or at all events, not to disturb the general well-being.
3. A deeper and more generally felt sense of the duty owed to infants and children by adults, not only to provide them, till capable of earning for themselves,

with adequate means of subsistence, but to give them that teaching and training which will lead to increase of wealth and enjoyment, and which will strengthen the desire to welcome and to master all new contributions to our old stock of knowledge and all improved combinations for turning knowledge to the best account.

4. The greater abundance and perfection of the contrivances and resources at man's disposal for communicating and recommending the discoveries and improved arrangements for human comfort, as soon as brought to light by one individual or nation, to all other individuals and nations.

. . . . . .

Another reward awaits students who seek their knowledge of the future exclusively through observation and experiment. They will arrive at a clearer appreciation of that part of the future which can be influenced by man, and be encouraged thereby to take rank among the causes at work to produce the better future which we prognosticate for the human race; and, at all events, not to be among the causes which retard the elevation of the masses, and obstruct that better future sure to come without, if not with, their assistance; after an interval, longer or shorter according to the number of human beings co-operating to impart to others the benefits of the advantages—foretaste of the better future in store for all— which a few only are now privileged to enjoy.

• • • • • •

Winwood Reade
The Martyrdom of Man (1872)

We live between two worlds; we soar in the atmosphere; we creep upon the soil; we have the aspirations of creators and the propensities of quadrupeds. There can be but one explanation of this fact. We are passing from the animal into a higher form; and the drama of this planet is in its second act.

· · · · · ·

We do not wish to extirpate religion from the life of man; we wish him to have a religion which will harmonise with his intellect, and which inquiry will strengthen, not destroy. We wish, in fact, to give him a religion, for now there are many who have none. We teach that there is a God, but not a God of the anthropoid variety, not a God who is gratified by compliments in prose and verse, and whose attributes can be catalogued by theologians. God is so great that he cannot be defined by us. God is so great that he does not deign to have personal relations with us human atoms that are called men. Those who desire to worship their Creator must worship him through mankind. Such it is plain is the scheme of Nature. We are placed under secondary laws, and these we must obey. To develop to the utmost our genius and our love, that is the only true religion. To do that which deserves to be written, to write that which deserves to be read, to tend the sick, to comfort the sorrowful, to animate the weary, to keep the temple of the body pure, to cherish the divinity within us, to be faithful to the intellect, to educate those powers which have been entrusted to our charge and to employ them in the service of humanity, that is all that we can do. Then our elements shall be dispersed and all is at an end. All is at an end for the unit, all is at an end for the atom, all is at an end for the speck of flesh and blood with the little spark of instinct which it calls its mind, but all is not at an end for the actual Man, the true Being, the glorious One. We teach that the soul is immortal; we teach that there is a future life; we teach that there is a Heaven in the ages far away; but not for us single corpuscles, not for us dots of animated jelly, but for the One of whom we are the elements, and who, though we perish, never dies, but grows from period to period and by the united efforts of single molecules called men, or of those cell-groups called nations, is raised towards the Divine power which he will finally attain. Our religion therefore is Virtue, our Hope is placed in the happiness of our posterity; our Faith is the Perfectibility of Man.

. . . . . .

You blessed ones who shall inherit that future age of which we can only dream; you pure and radiant beings who shall succeed us on the earth; when you turn back your eyes on us poor savages, grubbing in the ground for our daily bread, eating flesh and blood, dwelling in vile bodies which degrade us every day to a level with the beasts, tortured by pains, and by animal propensities, buried in gloomy superstitions, ignorant of Nature which yet holds us in her bonds; when you read of us in books, when you think of what we are, and compare us with yourselves, remember that it is to us you owe the foundation of your happiness and grandeur, to us who now in our libraries and laboratories and star-towers and dissecting-rooms and work-shops are preparing the materials of the human growth. And as for ourselves, if we are sometimes inclined to regret that our lot is cast in these unhappy days, let us remember how much more fortunate we are than those who lived before us a few centuries ago. The working man enjoys more luxuries to-day than did the King of England in the Anglo-Saxon times; and at his command are intellectual delights, which but a little while ago the most learned in the land could not obtain. All this we owe to the labours of other men. Let us therefore remember them with gratitude; let us follow their glorious example by adding something new to the knowledge of mankind; let us pay to the future the debt which we owe to the past.

. . . . . .

I give to universal history a strange but true title—*The Martyrdom of Man*. In each generation the human race has been tortured that their children might profit by their woes. Our own prosperity is founded on the agonies of the past. Is it therefore unjust that we also should suffer for the benefit of those who are to come? Famine, pestilence, and war are no longer essential for the advancement of the human race. But a season of mental anguish is at hand, and through this we must pass in order that our posterity may rise. The soul must be sacrificed; the hope in immortality must die. A sweet and charming illusion must be taken from the human race, as youth and beauty vanish never to return.

• • • • • •

Edward B. Tylor
"Primitive Society" (1873)

Of...more practical account than what we think of institutions of the past, is our approval or condemnation of the institutions we live among, our support in conservatism and our guide in reform. Such evidence as I have here brought forward may help to make good the claim of ethnology to aid in such practical judgments. We could not if we would wipe out history, and begin the world afresh on first principles. Whether we will or no, the morals and politics of future generations must bear, like our own, the stamp of their origin in primitive society. But our social science has a new character and power, inasmuch as we live near a turning point in the history of man-kind. The unconscious evolution of society is giving place to its conscious development; and the reformer's path of the future must be laid out on deliberate calculation from the track of the past.

• • • • • •

Herbert Spencer
Principles of Sociology (1874)

The advance from simple to the complex, through a process of successive differentiation, is seen alike in the earliest changes of the Universe to which we can reason our way back. And in the earliest changes we can inductively establish; it is seen in the geologic and climatic evolution of the Earth, and of every single organism on its surface; it is seen in the evolution of Humanity, whether contemplated in the civilized individual or in the aggregation of races; it is seen in the evolution of

Society...and in the evolution of all the endless concrete and abstract products of human activity.

• • • • • •

George P. Marsh
The Earth as Modified by Human Action (1874)

Note: Most of the text in the following passage is unchanged from an earlier, 1864 edition of the same book, titled Man and Nature. *This passage, therefore, could be considered the earliest in the anthology.*

Apart from the hostile influence of man, the organic and the inorganic world are...bound together by such mutual relations and adaptations as secure, if not the absolute permanence and equilibrium of both, a long continuance of the established conditions of each at any given time and place, or at least, a very slow and gradual succession of changes in those conditions. But man is everywhere a disturbing agent. Wherever he plants his foot, the harmonies of nature are turned to discords. The proportions and accommodations which insured the stability of existing arrangements are overthrown. Indigenous vegetable and animal species are extirpated, and supplanted by others of foreign origin, spontaneous production is forbidden or restricted, and the face of the earth is either laid bare or covered with a new and reluctant growth of vegetable forms, and with alien tribes of animal life. These intentional changes and substitutions constitute, indeed, great revolutions; but vast as is their magnitude and importance, they are, as we shall see, insignificant in comparison with the contingent and unsought results which have flowed from them.

The fact that, of all organic beings, man alone is to be regarded as essentially a destructive power, and that he wields energies to resist which Nature—that Nature whom all material life and all inorganic substance obey— is wholly impotent, tends to prove that, though living in physical nature, he is not of her, that he is of more exalted parentage, and belongs to a higher order of existences than those born of her womb and submissive to her dictates.

. . . . . .

Purely untutored humanity...interferes comparatively little with the arrangements of nature, and the destructive agency of man becomes more and more energetic and unsparing as he advances in civilization, until the impoverishment, with which his exhaustion of the natural resources of the soil is threatening him, at last awakens him to the necessity of preserving what is left, if not of restoring what has been wantonly wasted.

. . . . . .

The action of brutes upon the material world is slow and gradual, and usually limited, in any given case, to a narrow extent of territory. Nature is allowed time and opportunity to set her restorative powers at work, and the destructive animal has hardly retired from the field of his ravages before nature has repaired the damages occasioned by his operations. In fact, he is expelled from the scene by the very efforts which she makes for the restoration of her dominion. Man, on the contrary, extends his action over vast spaces, his revolutions are swift and radical, and his devastations are, for an almost incalculable time after he has withdrawn the arm that gave the blow, irreparable.

. . . . . .

The ravages committed by man subvert the relations and destroy the balance which nature had established between her organized and her inorganic creations; and she avenges herself upon the intruder, by letting loose upon her defaced provinces destructive energies hitherto kept in check by organic forces destined to be his best auxiliaries, but which he has unwisely dispersed and driven from the field of action...The earth is fast becoming an unfit home for its noblest inhabitant, and another era of equal human crime and human improvidence, and of like duration with that through which traces of that crime and that improvidence extend, would reduce it to such a condition of impoverished productiveness, of shattered surface, of climatic excess, as to threaten the depravation, barbarism, and perhaps even extinction of the species.

. . . . . .

Could this old world, which man has overthrown, be rebuilded, could human cunning rescue its wasted hillsides and its deserted plains from solitude or mere nomade occupation, from barrenness, from nakedness, and from insalubrity, and restore the ancient fertility and healthfulness of the Etruscan sea coast, the Campagna and the Pontine marshes, of Calabria, of Sicily, of the Peloponnesus and insular and continental Greece, of Asia Minor, of the slopes of Lebanon and Hermon, of Palestine, of the Syrian desert, of Mesopotamia and the delta of the Euphrates, of the Cyrenaica, of Africa proper, Numidia, and Mauritania, the thronging millions of Europe might still find room on the Eastern continent, and the main current of emigration be turned toward the rising instead of the setting sun.

But changes like these must await great political and moral revolutions in the governments and peoples by whom those regions are now possessed, but, especially, a command of pecuniary and of mechanical means not at present enjoyed by those nations, and a more advanced and generally diffused knowledge of the processes by which the amelioration of soil and climate is possible than now anywhere exists.

• • • • • •

J.E. Cairnes
"Social Evolution" (1875)

[A] time arrives in the progress of social development when societies of men become conscious of a corporate existence, and when the improvement of the conditions of this existence becomes for them an object of conscious and deliberate effort. At what particular stage in human history this new social force comes into play, we have no need here to inquire. What I am concerned to point out is that *it is a new social force*, wholly different in character from any which had hitherto helped to shape human destiny— wholly different also from those influences which have guided the unfolding either of the individual animal or of the species. We cannot, by taking thought, add a cubit to our stature. The species, in undergoing the process of improvement, is wholly unconscious of the influences that are determining its career. It is not so with human evolution. Civilized mankind are aware of the changes taking place in their social condition, and do consciously and deliberately take measures for its improvement.

• • • • • •

Frederic Harrison
"A Few Words About the Nineteenth Century" (1882)

There are...two ways in which a sudden flood of mechanical inventions embarrasses and endangers civilisation in the very act of advancing it. Science, philosophy, education, become smothered with the volume of materials before they have learned to use them, bewildered by the very multitude of their opportunities. Art, manners, culture, taste, suffer by the harassing rapidity into which life is whirled on from old to new fashion, from old to new interest, until the nervous system of the race itself is agitated and weakened by the never-ending rattle...Rest and fixity are essential to thought, to social life, to beauty; and a growing series of mechanical inventions making life a string of dissolving views is a bar to rest and fixity of any sort.

And if this restless change weakens the thought, the culture, and the habits of those who have leisure or wealth, it degrades and oppresses the life of those who labour and suffer, for their old habits of life are swept away before their new habits of life are duly prepared; and the increased resources of society are found in practice to be increased opportunities for the skilful to make themselves masters of the weak.

. . . . . .

[I]n an age of sudden material expansion, the forces that drive on the new phases in special lines are abnormally raised to fever heat, whilst those which in ordinary times are active to preserve the type are routed, abashed, and bewildered. In the long run the course of Order will rally again; but for the moment it is asked to do its work in what is something like an invasion or an earthquake. We have hardly yet got so far as to recognise that the sudden acquisition of vast material resources is not only a great boon to humanity, but also a tremendous moral, social, and even physical and intellectual experiment. Society is a most subtle organization; and we are apt to lose sight of the fact that an unlimited supply of steam power, or electric power, is not necessarily pure gain. The progress achieved in the external conditions of life within the last hundred years is no doubt greater than any recorded in human history. It is obvious that other kinds of progress have advanced at no such express speed. But, until all kinds of human energy get into more harmonious proportion, cantatas to the nineteenth century will continue to pall upon the impartial mind.

Socially, morally, and intellectually speaking, an era of extraordinary changes is an age that has cast on it quite exceptional duties. A child might as well play with a steam-engine or an electric machine, as we could prudently accept our material triumphs with a mere "rest and be thankful." To decry steam and electricity, inventions and products, is hardly more foolish than to deny the price which civilisation itself has to pay for the use of them. There are forces at work now, forces more unwearied than steam, and brighter than the electric arc, to rehumanise the dehumanised members of society; to assert the old immutable truths; to appeal to the old indestructible instinct; to recall beauty; forces yearning for rest, grace, and harmony; rallying all that is organic in man's social nature, and proclaiming the value of spiritual life over material life. But there never was a century in human history when these forces had a field so vast before them, or issues so momentous on their failure or their success. There never was an age when the need was so urgent for synthetic habits of thought, systematic education, and a common moral and religious faith. There is much to show that our better genius is awakened to the task. Stupefied with smoke, and stunned with steam-whistles, there was a moment when the century listened with equanimity to the vulgarest of its flatterers. But if Machinery were really its last word, we should all be rushing violently down a steep place, like the herd of swine.

• • • • • •

"A Misconception of History" (Editorial) (1884)

Is there any truth in the very general belief that during the period which has elapsed since the beginning of the French Revolution in 1789, now ninety-five years, or almost a century ago, the progress of events in the world of human life has gone on with a rapidity unknown in former ages? We think, on the whole, that this is an error—that the rapidity of the march of events does not vary much from age to age, and that what is peculiar to the present age is not the fact of rapid change, but the consciousness of it. Lord Macaulay says (we quote from memory):—"There is nothing new in the sufferings of the poor and the degradation of the criminal; what is new is the benevolence that concerns itself with them;" and we believe it is equally true that what is new in the nineteenth century is not the fact of change and progress in political society, but the social self-consciousness which takes note of them…certainly society is in our time conscious of itself, its own wants, diseases, and sins, in a degree in which it never was before.

• • • • • •

Edward J. Lowell
Response to "A Misconception of History" (1884)

It may make little difference, at least to the speculative philosopher in his arm-chair, that the peasant is a little warmer, a little fatter, a good deal more secure; that the poor are a little happier, and that on the whole they may enjoy their happiness a little longer. But one change the philosopher is bound to notice. The peasant has, if ambitious, acquired a new hope. If he be restless he may seek a change, and none can prevent him. A door has been opened to talent and ambition. The door was never absolutely closed; and it does not always lead anywhere; but it is open wider than ever before, and the prospect to be seen through it by strong eyes is broader.

Now, I am not aware that any change similar to this, or equal to it in importance, has taken place in the position or the prospects of the mass of people in Europe within historical times. It is a change rather moral than material.

…Was there any advance in the seventeenth and eighteenth centuries which correspond to the spread of popular education in the nineteenth? To find any change in the condition of the human mind comparable to this in importance, must we not go back to the Renascence of the fifteenth century, or at least to the Reformation of the sixteenth? And have not the inventions of the last fifty years, and especially the improved means of travel and diffusion of views, done something to enlarge the not over-broad minds of the industrial and trading classes? Was there any corresponding improvement between 1600 and 1800? And has not the discovery of anaesthetics, delivering us not only from the most severe forms of pain, but from the fear of them, added to the sum of happiness of the human race to an extent to which no previous improvement in the condition of human affairs has added to it?

...[I]f we compare the condition of the non-combatants in the invaded countries in the Franco-Prussian or the American Civil wars, on the one hand, with that of non-combatants in the wars of the eighteenth century on the other, it seems to me that we shall recognise a greater improvement during the last hundred years than during many centuries before...

...That the changes above-mentioned were preparing before 1789, there can be no doubt—no event in history stands by itself and disconnected; but it is since that date that they have manifested themselves, and had their effect on the mass of European mankind, and I think we may, therefore, hold that "the progress of events in the world of human life has gone on," during the century that is just passing away, with a rapidity greater than that attained during the two centuries which immediately preceded it, and probably "with a rapidity unknown in former ages."

• • • • • •

Jane Hume Clapperton

Scientific Meliorism and the Evolution of Happiness (1885)

The nineteenth century stands, I believe, at the threshold of
a new form of social life, and on the eve of a fresh departure.
Hitherto the race has stumbled forward, fighting blindly,
struggling manfully for life. Now the epoch before us is one
of consciousness—the open-eyed, dignified manhood of
our Power, possession, both are ours; we only pause for
knowledge, which will enable us to apply them to the good
and happiness of all. The struggle that goes on within the
nation is unworthy of its manhood. I do not mean that work
will ever cease—far from it. Consciousness of what true
happiness consists in, in the case of vigorous and social
human beings, must bring to light this fact: that "the finest
pleasures of life are to be found in the world of action," and
voluntary work will therefore never lose its charm. But
compulsion in our work, the bond of mastership and
servitude—the fierce inhuman struggle to obtain a share of
work, when aptitude and willingness exist—these will
certainly subside, and classes now at strife will find new
social joys in peaceful and industrial combination. To make
forecast of what we may anticipate, however, is not my
present purpose. My aim is purely practical. By the study
of evolution I think it possible to guide the thoughtful and
earnest in our midst to personal conduct which will tend to
bring about a happier social state.

· · · · · ·

My brave compatriots!—and by this term I address myself
specially to women, for my sex in this generation is
extremely brave—we fight for our rights, we step fearlessly
into the arena of public life and enter the lists with men in
so far as they will permit us; we speak boldly of subjects on

which our grandmothers kept silence; shall we be daunted by the magnitude of any task to which Nature calls us? She calls us loudly in this age to scientific reforms; she exposes to our eyes the hidden errors of the past; she makes us keenly feel the imperfection of human character within us and around us; she shows us unconscious evolution everywhere entering upon a conscious stage, in which man, in the van of circumstance, will shape the course for future humanity. It is absolutely essential that we should perceive the path of evolution, if we propose, with open-eyed intelligence, to aid evolution. I have in previous chapters used a figurative expression, viz. that we may take the forces of evolution into our hands, and apply them to our purpose in hastening the rapidity of their action. But we can never alter the path or direction of advance, and unless our action is in harmony with or (let us say) sets in the same direction as, the main force, we shall only foolishly oppose nature and stultify our own pygmy efforts. The *main force* of progression is, and must continue to be, purely automatic—a mighty irresistible movement of unconscious evolution, tending in a definite direction. It is the part of conscious intelligence, as an *evolution agency*, to ascertain the direction and study carefully the numerous, varied subsidiary forces that play important, although unconscious, parts in the general phenomena.

. . . . . .

Standing as we do at the beginning of an epoch of Conscious Evolution, the vista before Religion is indeed vast and magnificent, its work enormous. It has to reconcile the heart, and put into the hand of man the golden thread of science which will guide him in the labyrinth of life. It has to disclose all the grovelling instincts of humanity, and show the scientific method of their sure destruction. It has to nurse the nobler instincts, and to promote the rapid birth of the germs of a perfected Humanity. It has to make its way into every social channel, and reclaim the forces springing from unselfish emotion, that through mistaken aims and means are only producing social disorder. It has to call man's attention, engrossed in the taming of the Titans—that is, the subjugation of the material forces of external nature—to the infinitely subtler and more important task of procuring health, physical, spiritual, and social, for the world at large. It has to reveal the new heaven and the new earth, and to inspire mankind with the faith, the energy, the indomitable will, to move in that direction, "Let us be worthy of the opportunity which is ours. Future generations may be happier than we are in many respects, but for the heroic pleasures—the pleasures of devotion to an ideal, which shall not be realized till the grass has long grown over our graves—there never was, and perhaps never will be, a time equal to that in which we live."

. . . . . .

Unconscious evolution has carried us forward from savagery through many transitions to a state of civilization which, although grossly imperfect and partial, contains within it a new element of advance, capable of intensifying the action of blind evolutionary forces and immensely increasing their momentum. Not universally, but here and there throughout society, the power of reason in Humanity has become strong, and, aided by a scientific knowledge of man and the conditions of his life, this psychic force—the conscious element in evolution, the power of design—may initiate a fresh departure. Reason must be directed, however, to the invention of an effective policy of

Meliorism which so combines the practical methods of reform, as that each will add strength to all and the result prove a powerful factor of change in the society on which it is brought to bear. Scientific ideas of the universe and the nature of man, and an accurate acquaintance with the facts of our national history, are essential to the creation of such a policy.

· · · · · ·

Now, the conscious element in evolution is as yet far too weak to alter general society much for the better; and the State is wholly unfit to reorganize society. Conscious evolution, however, if socially localized, i.e. centred in groups of human beings within general society, becomes at once capable of effective action. Whilst Meliorism must present ideally an "organization of all facts, forces, and phenomena into an orderly and connected system," its practice during a transition epoch will primarily be carried out in individual groups, by clusters of select human beings whose high standard of intellectual and moral attainment fits them for union in domestic life under conditions of voluntary socialism.

• • • • • •

Francis C. Montague
The Limits of Individual Liberty (1885)

The conscious and reflecting individual is the child of the conscious and reflecting society...Such a society has a moral as well as a physical life. It partakes in progress as well as in evolution. In the state of nature, society determined the individual, and was determined by him.

The individual and the social development were inseparable. This mutual dependence and this intimate union survive, but are transformed in the age of reflection. The moral and rational society, the State, is aware that it is what its citizens are. It acknowledges the duty of doing what it can for their welfare. And the thinking and responsible individual finds not only that society has made him what he is, but also that he can improve himself only by improving his society. In place of an individual and a community linked by a mere physical necessity, acting and reacting without will or conscience, and evolving one another by mere force of appetite, we have a citizen and a State united by ties of love and duty, conscious of the way in which the one affects the other, and each attaining to a better life by endeavouring to better the other.

• • • • • •

E.P. Powell
Our Heredity from God (1887)

You will find that there is no question of life, or of thought, of religion, history, philosophy, of social science or politics, that does not seek its solution in evolution.

. . . . . .

The most important of moral needs is that the general interdependence of nature shall be supplemented in man by an appreciation of his responsibility in shaping this relation, by his own volition, for ethical ends. Societies for the suppression of cruelty to animals, all honest efforts to ameliorate the conditions of poverty, are thus man's contribution to the co-operative good-will of life energies.

. . . . . .

The alphabet, the press, the steamship, mark propulsions of such an extraordinary nature; but never has human thought speeded with such continuous leaps of inspired progress as during our own age of science. Freed from the necessity of conforming our knowledge to a preconceived theory of causation, mind has achieved in one century the work of a millennium.

. . . . . .

A perfect world is the struggle of imperfect beings toward betterment...Evolution without beginning, is also evolution without an end.

. . . . . .

Man is the fruit, but not the ripe fruit, of evolution...He is already a child of cosmical environments, but it does not yet appear what he shall be. He weaves now at the loom of his own destiny.

. . . . . .

Man himself stands so related, so faced, so inherently tending, as to constitute in himself a readable prophecy — not of perpetuity as he is or may be in the present life, but of higher states of being under better environments. He constitutes a positive and forceful bias of evolution in that direction and to that end. Evolution can not stop at man as he is. It is a process not only through an eternal past but through an eternal future; and the future ever will be, as the past ever has been, determined by the ethico-intelligent aim embodied in the process. Man constitutes a factor of this aim or purpose, an element of the determinative tendency of the future.

● ● ● ● ● ●

Catherine Helen Spence
"A Week in the Future" (1888)

For context, the following passage is from a novella written from the perspective of an imagined visit to the year 1988, one hundred years into the future.

And how did my new friends look on me? Kindly enough, but with some pity that I had been placed in such a barbarous age. Yet this barbarous age contained in it the germs of all that had been accomplished afterwards. It was the beginning of the age of conscious evolution. Before my day the race had stumbled forward, fighting blindly, struggling manfully for life. In common with thousands, nay with tens-of-thousands, I had entered the epoch of consciousness, the open-eyed, dignified manhood of humanity. We had power and passion, we only paused for knowledge, so as to apply these to the good and happiness of all. I looked back, and I saw the beginning of much that had been evolved in my own mind, and in the minds of others. I, myself, had done something, not much, but still somewhat towards those changes that others had worked more efficiently under more favorable circumstances to bring about.

• • • • • •

Minot J. Savage
"The Effects of Evolution on The Coming Civilization"
(1889)

This is not a dead universe, but a live one; and it is moving with tremendous power in certain definite directions. We can neither ignore this movement nor oppose it...If it is on an upward track, then we may hopefully co-operate with it; we may even hasten the coming of better days.

. . . . . .

I do not see how any intelligent believer in Evolution can despair. But if he be an intelligent believer, he will know that the first thing to be done is to find out which way things are tending...The force of evolution did not stop with intellect. It has climbed up into the moral. And to-day the ethical ideal is mightier than all muscle not only, but all brain. It dominates the nations...After a long contest with materialistic theories and tendencies, there is apparent a tremendous upheaval of the spiritual forces in man. It looks like an unfolding of spiritual tendencies and forces such as the world has never seen...The question now before us is as to what is the next step.

. . . . . .

A perfect society cannot be made out of the imperfect individuals. Rearrange them as you please, and so long as the materials are defective the defect will appear in the result. Forgetting this is the radical error in all those theories that propose some short cut to the "Coming Civilization," while men and women are left very much the same as they are now...Something, and I believe, very much, is possible, if only people will stop merely dreaming and, in the light of established principles, will go to work.

. . . . . .

I believe this old earth is capable of sustaining an ideal civilization—one as fair as the fairest that any most enthusiastic dreamer has dreamed. And I believe this wondrous race of ours, that has accomplished so much, is capable of realizing it. But it must be by facing facts, and by working along the lines of existing laws and forces. There is no magic about it, no short cut, no royal road. It is not to be learned in "six short and easy lessons"…So we shall not expect everything, or too much, all at once. If we can take the next step, we shall do well.

. . . . . .

These steps, then, society is competent to take. I see no other way. It must be by education, and so through increased mastery of the natural forces on the part of man, that the higher life must come. That which lifts the social level, creates in man higher wants, and so stimulates him to the production of ever more and more of those things in which real wealth consists, to the end that these wants may be supplied, — this and this only can help the race on the next step towards the "Coming Civilization." This is the lesson of all the past, and here is the prophecy of the future. Long and weary has been the way. But if Evolution teaches anything, it is tireless patience and deathless hope.

● ● ● ● ● ●

James Seth
"The Evolution of Morality" (1889)

Self-conscious evolution is essentially different from unconscious evolution, and the former cannot be stated in terms of the latter. While all lower life evolves by strict unconscious necessity, man, as self-conscious, is free from its dominion; and has the power consciously to help on, or consciously to hinder, the evolution.

● ● ● ● ● ●

Joseph Le Conte
"The Factors of Evolution" (1891)

[O]nly with the appearance of man, another entirely different and far higher factor was introduced, viz. *conscious, voluntary co-operation in the work of evolution*—a conscious voluntary *effort to attain an Ideal*. As already said, we call this a factor, but it is much more than a factor. It is another nature working in another world—the spiritual—and like physical nature using all factors, but in a new way and on a higher plane. In early stages man developed much as other animals, unconscious and careless whither he tended and therefore with little or no voluntary effort attain a higher stage. But this voluntary factor, this striving toward a goal or ideal, in the individual and in the race, increased more and more until in civilised communities of modern times it has become by far the dominant factor. Reason, instead of physical nature, takes control, though still using the same factors.

...With the appearance of reason in man another and far higher factor is introduced which in its turn assumes control, and not only again quickens the rate, but elevates the whole plane of evolution. This voluntary, rational factor not only assumes control itself, but transforms all other factors and uses them in a new way and for its own higher purposes.

This last is by far the greatest change which has ever occurred in the history of evolution. In organic evolution nature operates by necessary law without the voluntary co-operation of the thing evolving. In human progress man voluntarily co-operates with nature in the work of evolution and even assumes to take the process mainly into his own hands. Organic evolution is by *necessary* law, human progress by *free*, or at least by *freer*, law. Organic evolution is by a pushing upward and onward from below and behind, human progress by an aspiration, an attraction toward an ideal—a *pulling* upward and onward from above and in front.

· · · · · ·

Man's own effort is the chief factor in his own evolution. By virtue of his self-activity, and through the use of reason, man alone is able to rectify an error of direction and return again to the deserted way.

· · · · · ·

If it be true that reason must direct the course of human evolution, and if it be also true that selection of the fittest is the only method available for that purpose; then, if we are to have any race-improvement at all, the dreadful law of *destruction of the weak and helpless* must with Spartan firmness be carried out voluntarily and deliberately. Against such a course all that is best in us revolts. The use of the Lamarckian factors, on the contrary, is not attended with any such revolting consequences. All that we call education, culture, training, is by the use of these.

· · · · · ·

We have said that the new factor introduced with man is a voluntary co-operation in the process of evolution, a conscious upward striving toward a higher condition, a pressing forward toward an ideal. Man contrary to all else in nature is transformed, not in *shape* by external environment, but in *character by his own ideals*. Now this capacity of forming ideals and the voluntary pursuit of such ideals, whence comes it? When analysed and reduced to simplest terms, it is naught else than the consciousness in man and his relation to the infinite and the attempt to realise the divine ideal in human character.

• • • • • •

Carrie Chapman Catt
"Evolution and Woman's Suffrage" (1893)

[I]n centuries past, those who looked out upon the mild passions and conflicting events of their own times must have paused to say, I know not what all this means, I know not from whence these human discords come, nor whither they will tend. But to those who stand on the lofty of this new opinion born in our own century, the past has revealed its every secret. Every event has been explained. Every thread has been picked up and woven into a chain of perfect symmetry. We know to-day that the history of man has been an evolution. We know to-day that in response to the immutable laws of nature, step by step, as gently and as naturally as the unfolding of a blade of grass, every event has found its place.

This new opinion may well be called the great discovery of our century. It is revolutionizing thought in every line of life. It is modifying religious creeds, and political faiths. It is putting new ideas of human possibilities into all the governments of the world. It is filling the air over the heads of all the nations of earth with finer, grander, and loftier sentiments of human rights and liberties than any century before.

Evolution is not an hypothesis but an absolute proof that the "world does move"; that it moves ever onward and upward, that the path of men leads ever nearer and nearer the perfect and ideal. It points to the fact every century had its new habits of thought, its new reforms, its new inquiries and investigations, and every century has brought humanity nearer to truth and justice. Who is there then, who can prophesy the hope, the promise, the purpose which will be evolved out of future centuries? Who is there can read the possibilities of human liberty and happiness evolution will unfold?

Women have had their own individual evolution. I once knew of a man, a very little man, physically, and mentally, and morally. He was a very religious man and used always to go to church twice on Sunday accompanied by his wife. She invariably walked some little distance behind him. If she thought of something she wanted to say to him and should catch up with him, he would as invariably pause and with an imperious gesture would say, "Remember, remember, Mary Ann, three paces behind, three paces behind." Three paces behind, the women of the world have had their revolution out of the savagery of the past, into the light and freedom of the present. They stand three paces behind to-day. Yet the finest, and the grandest, and the loftiest sentiment hovering over the heads of all the advanced nations of earth is the advance of their women to their rightful plans [sic] by the side of their husbands, and fathers and sons. It is the finest sentiment because it demands the application of finest principles of justice; it is the grandest sentiment because it means the uplifting of the whole human race; it is the loftiest sentiment because it aims its attack on the oldest and best established prejudices of history.

And is the reform for which we stand to continue a sentiment in the clouds, or will it be caught and chained to custom and law? To know, we have to ask is our cause just. We ask this question and in reply every instinct of woman's individuality and self-respect, every principle of modern government, of common sense and common fairness comes to declare "it is just."

...[O]ut of all the centuries without one shade of doubt within its voice thunders back, "it shall be." The only question is <u>when</u> and <u>how</u>.

We ask when? Evolution answers "Now." It is a sub-law of the great universal law of evolution that whenever nature demands a new development, it comes.

. . . . . .

We shall hear in the course of the next six months much of the material progress of the world. It has been marvellous. No century has witnessed such luxury, such elegance, such display, yet the statisticians of the world assure us that no century has seen more misery and poverty and suffering than ours. We shall be told there has been no time when there has been such determined, organized effort and the expenditure of so much money to help humanity, for this is a generous century as well; yet the statisticians tell us vice and crime has more than kept pace with all this progress. We shall hear how the aspirations of this century are being constantly directed to new reforms and to new efforts to help mankind, yet the statistician assures us, never before have so many gone down to drunkard's graves, never were there so many insane and idiots, never so much unfortunate humanity. These are phases of our modern life of which we shall not hear. Yet they are real facts of our existence and must be counted in the measure of the advance of our evolution.

What does it mean? Why are these things so? It is because our civilization is strong and well-developed along all the lines of men's keenest interests, wealth and law and

58

commerce. They are weak along the lines of women's keenest interests, protection of the individual and the home.

. . . . . .

Upon this 19th Century Evolution has laid the moral responsibility for woman's ballot and it will come. Evolution, the greatest truth discovered in our century, is on our side. With that great truth as our comforter and guide, let us not turn back to the sad history of woman's degradation but look only to the future where already the whole sky is ablaze with the promise of coming liberty for woman and broader opportunities for a "whole humanity."

We ask how this sentiment is to be caught out of the clouds and crystallized into law and custom. Evolution answers. By the same means which has wrought every change in society—Work...Work and we shall win for evolution, the law of the universe, has decreed it.

• • • • • •

Rev. Josiah Strong
The New Era or The Coming Kingdom (1893)

Let us glance hastily at some of the more significant changes which have taken place during the past century and note their meaning.

1st. Changes which may be called physical. There is nothing more fundamental touching the circumstances which affect all human beings than time and space. They condition all human activities and relationships, and hence to change them is to affect all human activities and relationships. This is the reason that steam and electricity have had so profound an influence on modern civilization...It is as if the earth had been, in two or three generations, reduced to a much smaller scale and set spinning on its axis at a far greater speed. As a result, men have been brought into much closer relations and the world's rate of progress has been wonderfully quickened...By reason of the increased use of communication new ideas are more speedily popularized, public opinion more quickly formed and more readily expressed; both thought and action are stimulated; reforms are sooner accomplished, and great changes of every sort are crowded into as many years as once they would have required generations or even centuries.

. . . . . .

Progress has not been uniform or constant, but no one can question that civilization is on a higher plane now than formerly. We have better laws, better institutions, higher moral standards, more of liberty and less of lawlessness and violence; and these changes show a change in man himself.

. . . . . .

There are reasons for believing that the world's progress toward a perfect society is to be much more rapid in the future than it has been in the past...The development of the individual and the organization of society were the two fundamental principles in the history of civilization, the two lines along which the progress of the race could be traced...The progress of civilization has been slow because the conditions most favorable to the development of one of these principles have been least favorable to the development of the other. *It is of the utmost significance that now for the first time in the history of the race the same causes are favorable to the development of both.*

. . . . . .

In a word, these great forces which are now exerting so profound an influence on civilization are far more favorable to organization than the conditions which produced the vast organizations of Asia, and at the same time much more stimulating to the individual than those conditions which produced the individualism of Europe. Surely such a change, harnessing together to the chariot of the world's progress these two principles which for thousands of years have drawn, now one and then the other, but never together, and often against each other, is so profoundly significant that it marks nothing less than the beginning of a NEW ERA in the history of the race.

. . . . . .

This is not the first age of the world when there has been a widespread discontent, but it means more in this age than it ever meant before, because there is greater popular intelligence. An intelligent discontent will not suffer in dumb despair; it has resources, means of expressing itself and of enforcing its demands. It can agitate, and educate public opinion. It knows enough of the progress of the world in the past to hope for the future, and it is easy for hope to purpose and achieve.

. . . . . .

The great changes of the nineteenth century have been beginnings rather than endings…they have prepared the way for still greater probable changes in the twentieth century. We have seen that popular discontent is deep-seated and widespread, that it is not likely to be temporary, that it will be satisfied with nothing less than the most important and far-reaching economic and social changes, and that the restless masses are the power which will determine our future.

. . . . . .

The most powerful tendency of the times is centripetal. It is profoundly influencing production and distribution—industries of all sorts—and the movement of populations. So general a tendency toward combination, organization, centralization, indicates...nothing less than a new evolution of civilization, the beginning of a higher organization of society, made possible by steam and electricity and the higher development of the individual.

● ● ● ● ● ●

A Free Lance (a.k.a. F.H. Perry-Coste),
Towards Utopia (1894)

Everybody is familiar with the conception of Utopia; and many among us believe that social evolution will presently culminate in an Utopia where all shall be good, wise, cultured, and affluent: but, whilst we have many popular imaginative descriptions of this *completed* future state, it is perhaps somewhat less usual to enquire what precisely are some of the individual *natural* processes by which that happy consummation can be brought about; what, if anything, can be done by us of to-day to hasten the progress; *and what price, if any, must be paid for Utopia.*

. . . . . .

Of one thing we are convinced—and to this we need fear little contradiction—that the prime factor in any revolution, or rather renovation, of society, must ever be a change in the ideas, feelings, sympathies, and aspirations of the individuals who compose that society; the first step towards any advance must be to thoroly change the *mental atmosphere* in which we live; given so much, and the rest *must* follow, for the world of men is ruled by thoughts and feelings.

. . . . . .

Our only object…is to endeavour to descry some few of the landmarks that point the path to Utopia; and, once and for all, let us say that our conception of Utopia is *not* as the best imaginable world, *but* the best possible. Humanity can never transcend the conditions of existence; and while death exists, Perfect Happiness is unattainable. Our concern is therefor with the least possible imperfect; and it necessarily follows that, to our thinking, Utopia can be reached only after a long journey through semi-Utopia.

. . . . . .

[H]ow do any changes come to naturally occur? What is the forerunner and cause of every social or constitutional reform: what else but a previous moment of thought and feeling? The reform was made a certainty at that moment when, in the majority of the people, there was implanted a perception of its necessity, or a strong impulse toward the change: always and everywhere the *first necessity then is to revolutionise the thoughts* and to render a given *idea* familiar and agreeable…The whole change to be healthy, and to be effectual, must be a naturally evolved product: but we may vastly assist the one half of the evolutionary process, by educating men to desire it; a very main obstacle to social advance will then have been removed.

• • • • • •

Albion W. Small and George E. Vincent
An Introduction to the Study of Society (1894)

Is there…a social consciousness as distinguished from that of the individual? May an act be conscious from the standpoint of the social unit, and, nevertheless, unconscious on the part of society as a whole?…We believe that the distinction between individual and collective consciousness is clearly observable in the most familiar of social phenomena, and is fully recognized in practice, if not in theory, by those who are trying to modify social arrangements…

Unconsciousness is a conspicuous characteristic of social activities and institutions. Individuals seek the satisfaction of their own desires with little or no thought of the relations which their acts sustain to the total life of society. Although in performing social tasks individuals usually avoid infringement of each other's spheres of activity, and thus conform to a certain system of cooperation, they do not, in most things, have a reasoned and conscious plan of collective action. From this it follows that many institutions are largely unconscious social growths, which have developed through long periods of time. The family institution, the industrial system, language itself, have been produced gradually and not according to preconceived ideals.

Social unconsciousness, as DeGreef has pointed out, characterizes the phenomena which are connected with the lower human wants, and find expression in propagation and in production and distribution. The functions of sociability, education, and discipline display a certain degree of social consciousness, while in politics society at last assumes a more or less reasoned control of its own activities and attempts to direct them toward a definite goal.

The reforming enthusiast is prone to bewail the unconsciousness of society, but this very trait is manifestly one of the economies of nature. If it were not for this more or less reflex character of social functions, if collective reason were compelled constantly to deal with the manifold and complex conditions which society presents, irresolution and anarchy would prevail. Yet...consciousness has an important part to play in social progress...

The development of society exhibits a succession of states of consciousness which, finding expression in written or unwritten laws, or in modifications of institutions, fade away. The changes in activities, arrangements, and standards once consciously made, are soon consolidated and become points of departure for still further readjustments. The economy of such a procedure is manifest. Reflex, unreasoned actions are promptly performed with the minimum of effort. Consciousness serves to modify and improve the nature of structure or function, then gives place to reflex action.

Thus it is evident that the stimulation of social consciousness is a matter of great concern to those who are engaged in tasks of social amelioration or reformation. In the last analysis, it is by this means only that important and genuine changes can be effected. Yet the difficulties and limitations in creating social consciousness may be easily underestimated and cause serious disappointment to sanguine philanthropists.

• • • • • •

Blanche Leppington
"The Debrutalization of Man" (1895)

Man has glimpsed his future in the magic mirror of his past. He knows now what Nature (if we are to use no greater name than Nature) has been doing for him all along; he guesses what she is going on to do. Is her aim his aim? He is now the living witness of his own evolution: must he not be henceforth a conscious agent in directing it? He must follow her methods then. He must elect, reject, conserve, suppress. He must help her to prune what is disproportionate, to evoke what is latent, to subordinate the lower to the higher, to refine and elaborate the crude and elementary shapes of new and nobler growths.

• • • • • •

Lewis G. Janes
"Cosmic Evolution, as Related to Ethics" (1895)

From a formless gas to a solid globe; from the theatre of fierce plutonic activities to a condition where such activities are rare and exceptional; from an inanimate mass to a home for manifold forms of life; from coarser to finer forms of vegetation; from moneron to ape and from ape to man; from savagery to barbarism and from barbarism to civilization: this has been the life-history of our little world—the sole object-lesson from which we have the right to judge of the actual nature and tendency of cosmic evolution. Here is the large fact of progress, which is by no means reversed or seriously discounted by the incidental fact that this progress has not been serial, but rhythmical, that occasional and local degeneration has been an accompaniment of the general evolutionary process.

And now, at the culmination of the great cosmic process, man stands forth—child of the great World-Mother—a being capable of reflection, investigation and rational volition as a guide to his own activities; a tremendous factor henceforward in the evolutionary process, who by thought, married to deeds, cannot only change his own stature—contrary to scriptural suggestion—but can form his own character, modify his environment, and vastly help or hinder the progress of the world. Nay, he *is* doing it, whether he will or not—for evil if not for good—wasting the richness which affluent Nature has placed in his hands by unwise prodigality, wasting his own life by heedlessly devoting it to selfish or unworthy ends, or wisely enlarging it and the world's prosperity by a well-considered balance of economy and expenditure of vital resource in the service of his fellows. A creature like man cannot be a mere make-weight in the economy of Nature; he must *tell*, either one way or the other—for good or for ill.

. . . . . .

It is the great virtue of the evolutionary ethic that it calls man from the cloud-land of metaphysical speculation, and seeks to enlighten his intellect and guide his steps by appeals to the scientifically ascertained facts of human experience, and the laws by which they are governed. Back to Nature—not in her statical aspects, as dreamed by Rousseau and the Enlightenment Century philosophers, but in her dynamical and evolutionary aspects—must we ever go for ethical guidance, encouragement, and inspiration.

• • • • • •

Mariott Brosius
"The Medical Profession and the State" (1895)

With the increase of population and the growth of
civilization the social organism increases in complexity and
the difficulties of government multiply. The results of the
evolutionary movement of society deepen the obscurity
and increase the hardness of the problems submitted for
human solution. Situations must, indeed, be hard to meet
when the complex movements which evolve them are so
hard to tell about. Herbert Spencer's formula presents a
collection of words which, though not of a character to
"shatter the teeth of a crocodile," yet paralyze the mind of
a common man. Learned doctors, of course, comprehend
these words when they hear them, namely, "a change from
a definite, coherent homogeneity, to an indefinite,
incoherent homogeneity through continuous
differentiations and integrations." That tells you in a plain
way what is going on in society...

This occult process is going on continuously, and,
while it augments human perplexity and increasingly taxes
human intelligence, it is supposed that, in some manner, at
some time, by a mysterious power residing in the nature of
things, society will arrive at perfection. Male lecturers are
discoursing on the "New Woman" and female on the "New
Man," and, as pictured from the respective points of view,
they are superior creatures. It is a splendid thing to believe
that the human race will one day flower into perfect beings
who can live by the golden rule...The time that Herbert
Spencer sees through his evolutionary glasses, when man

will be so happily adjusted to his environment that righteousness will everywhere prevail, and conscience, no longer necessary, will be dispensed with, will never come. An awakened conscience, a resolute will, an enlightened mind, and a loyal devotion to duty will be the chief agencies in human progress until the end of it...

Seeing how bewildering is the attempt to convey an idea of the nature of evolution will help to make us suitably sensible of the accumulating difficulties which will be presented in the course of our social and political development, and of the necessity of a progressively increasing accumulation of intelligence in the body of our citizenship, to keep its equipment in any degree commensurate with the exigencies which will call it into use.

The people of the United States are approaching, if they are not already face to face, with social and political problems of extreme gravity. Problems which but a short while ago we contemplated only with enlightened curiosity now lie like lions across our path. Carlyle said, half a century ago, "that America's battle is yet to fight; that new spiritual pythons, enormous megatheriums as were ever born of mud, loom, huge and hideous, in the twilight-future." The pythons and megatheriums which are glaring at us with ferocious eyes to-day were not born of mud, but of the ceaseless and sometimes tumultuous striving of the human family for something better,—a reaching out in the dark for succor, from what they feel to be the cruelty of inequality in the distribution of the benefits of civilization. If we are to find a solution for these stupendous problems we must be wiser than our fathers. We cannot guide the ship of state in the tumultuous sea of the future by the observations of the past. The growth of intelligence, public reason, and social insight must keep pace with the conditions which require their exercise. We must know how to treat popular discontent,—when with repressive laws and when with measures of conciliation and relief; how to retire old institutions to make way for new ones; how to make the changes which are inevitable, made necessary by the progress of society, and not to be resisted.

• • • • • •

Henry Dyer
Evolution of Industry (1895)

The recognition of the processes of evolution in the natural and physical worlds, of the gradual progress from the simple to the complex, from the indeterminate to the determinate, from the uniform to the varied, from the homogeneous to the heterogeneous, and of successive integrations as the steps of this progress, has led to the application of the same methods and principles in psychology, morality and sociology, although, as we shall see presently, when we are dealing with intelligent and ethical man, great care requires to be taken in making analogies with the phenomena of the physical and natural worlds.

· · · · · ·

Without...conscious co-operation and modification by man of the evolutionary forces in action, survival may often be the reward of anti-social characteristics, cunning, violence, unscrupulousness; or it may be due to social arrangements for which the individuals most concerned are not directly responsible, for all these may be modified or completely changed by intelligent and ethical human effort.

. . . . . .

While we may give up our imperfect conception of God, we cannot abandon all belief in a purpose, an intention, a finality of some sort, which always has been, and still is being, manifested in the universe and in the evolution of human destiny. The part which man plays in working out this destiny is most important, for he can, either individually or collectively, modify his development in any desired direction by changing the nature of his environment. The character of his ideals, his sense of moral duty, and his efforts for the welfare of others, may reverse the conditions which are found in nature, and may substitute the principle of self-sacrifice for that of selfish struggle.

. . . . . .

What is true of individuals is also true of organisations in society, and in fact of society as a whole. They must not be allowed to drift under the influence of blind forces, or be subordinated to selfish ends, but must be consciously dominated by a social ideal which will lead to the welfare of the greatest number. That is to say, the environments both of individuals and of communities must be consciously moulded in such a manner as to lead to the highest individual and collective welfare...

It is evident that the chief problem of to-day is to balance fairly the demands of the individual and of his environment. Individual progress and improvement of environment must go on simultaneously, and...the formula of the relation of individual human life to environment must be different from that which applies to irrational animals. Man not only modifies, but to a large extent makes, his own environment; and all experience shows that an active and strong mind, imbued with high ideals of life and duty, can rise above even degrading social conditions. In the same way groups of men and women or communities can make, or at least profoundly modify, their environments, and as individuals need ideals at which to aim, so also societies require to look beyond the mere demands of to-day or even of to-morrow, and to plan their organisation in such a manner as will conduce to the healthy development of the great masses of the people.

. . . . . .

Of this we may rest assured, that the triumphs of science and industry are the most powerful factors of the age, and we cannot get rid of them even if we wished…The problem before us is to utilise them that they will not degrade any portion of the community, but will enable each one to live a healthy, noble life, and society to realise an order far beyond our highest ideals. The mechanical development of the nineteenth century was a very necessary step in the evolution of society. That of the twentieth will bring us still nearer to the conditions which prophets have foretold, of which poets have sung, and which are now almost within our grasp if we deliberately try to obtain them. We cannot bring back the old order of things in the industrial and commercial world, but we ought to welcome and understand the new, not as it has been forced upon a world animated by self-seeking and greed, but as it might be when regulated by the wisdom and generosity of those who prize justice as the first necessity with their fellow men. Modern social conditions are forcing the need for such an ideal upon all who look beneath the surface of our boasted progress.

. . . . . .

It is quite evident that the old political parties are disappearing, and that their places are being taken by others who profess to make the improvement of the social and economic conditions of the people their chief aim. Unfortunately the measures they propose and attempt to carry out are very often of an opportunist nature, and may delay the real solutions of the problems with which we are confronted. Hence the necessity for an education in the duties of Citizenship. As this develops and people are trained to think out the solutions of the problems, they will endeavour to become conscious helpers in the evolution of a nobler society than that of which they presently form a part...

. . . . . .

While it is unwise to indulge too much in the framing of complete Utopias, a moderate exercise of the imagination is very necessary so that the mind may rise above many of the low and sordid views of life and its possibilities too often held at present. As the evolution proceeds, the accomplishment of any part of the hopes of those who are intelligently and earnestly working for the welfare of humanity will open new vistas of progress, in which not only new problems will be presented, but also methods of solution which are at present undreamt of, and which will probably indicate possibilities which are far beyond the highest ideals of any Utopia which has ever been painted.

• • • • • •

Charles W. Dabney, Jr.
Commencement Address (1896)

The harmonious and equitable evolution of man does not mean that every man must be educated just like his fellow. The harmony is within each individual. That community is most highly educated in which each individual has attained the maximum of his possibilities in the direction of his peculiar talents and opportunities. This produces not a Procrustean sameness, but an infinite diversity in purpose and potentiality. The perfect education is one which tunes every string on each human instrument. Each musical instrument must, they tell us, in order to develop the most perfect sounds, be tuned separately by a sympathetic spirit and a skillful hand. A nation of men and women all perfectly educated would be like a grand orchestra of such musical instruments, all perfectly tuned. There are hundreds of instruments and players, and yet each instrument can make its own peculiar music. All are necessary to produce the grand symphony. An orchestra made up entirely of like instruments would be no orchestra at all. So the life of each man and woman may be a melody, and whether it is the loud-pealing hymn of the cathedral organ, or the soft pleading of the Spanish lover's guitar as he sings his serenade, it makes little difference what instrument one plays so he makes music in his life.

• • • • • •

Elisée Reclus
"The Progress of Mankind" (1896)

While geography conquered space, and thus made it possible for mankind to become conscious of itself from one end of the world to the other, the historian, turning towards the past, conquered time. The human race, which is unifying itself from one end of the world to the other, is equally attempting to realise itself under a form which embraces all the ages. This is a second conquest not less important than the first. All anterior civilisations, even the prehistoric, are henceforth more or less known to us, and consequently can, in a certain sense, be incorporated into the life of modern societies. By the succession of periods, which we can now study as a synoptical table unfolding itself according to the perfect logic of events, we cease to live merely in the flying moment; we embrace the past in the ages retraced by the annalists. In this way we detach ourselves from the strict line of development indicated by our environment and our race, and we see unrolled before us all the paths, parallel or divergent, that other fractions of humanity have followed. The ways are open to us, and we feel obliged to enter them, for any example given by other men, our brothers, must appeal to our genius of imitation. As our horizon is enlarged, in time as well as in space, a greater number of models for study crowd round us, and among them there is much to awaken in us the desire to resemble them in one part or another of their ideal. In moving about, and in modifying ourselves, we have lost a certain part of our acquisitions, and now we may ask ourselves whether it is not possible to recover all the baggage abandoned at the different stages of our long Odyssey through time.

A third conquest of civilisation is the most obvious, and the ordinary panegyrists of the present day are therefore eager to insist upon it—the prodigious development of modern industry, due to the discoveries of men of learning and to the practical genius of the innumerable Prometheuses, bearers of the sacred fire, who spring from the school and the factory. On the other hand, the over-cultured, the poets, declaring themselves in love with antique simplicity, affect to despise all this utilitarian progress of society, though they deign to make use of it to their own advantage; and if they seek mediæval objects for the ornamentation of their dwellings, they appreciate on every important occasion in life rapid locomotion and the almost instantaneous transmission of voice and thought. Whatever disdain the pessimist may bestow upon this prodigious growth of human forces, the sincere man is struck with admiration at these machines, which have more than doubled the power of human work, and given to our life so great intensity of action. The active worker can henceforth condense into his short life of sixty to eighty years, more work than one of his ancestors, reduced to his own force alone, could have accomplished in a thousand years.

. . . . . .

[T]he old adage, "Know thyself," has never been so near to realisation; for one can only know oneself by comparison with another, and in these days the dissection of the human being from an intellectual and moral point of view is pursued in a systematic manner with astonishing acuteness of discernment. Psychology has become an exact science, and character novels, a style formerly unknown, have taken a rank of very high order in contemporary literature. Man, in learning more narrowly to scrutinize himself, even in parts of his nature until recently beyond his consciousness, discovers for each of the acquisitions and revelations of his own being corresponding wants; his ideal grows indefinitely in proportion to the improvement of his mind and the sensibility of his heart.

. . . . . .

Thus admirably furnished with tools by its progress in the knowledge of space and of time, of the intimate nature of things and of man himself, is mankind at the present time prepared to approach the capital problem of its existence, the realisation of a collective ideal? Certainly. The work, if not of assimilation, at least of appropriation of the earth is nearly terminated, to the profit of the nations called civilised, who have become by this very fact the nurses and educators of the world; there are no longer any barbarians to conquer; and, consequently, the directing classes will soon be without the resource of employing abroad their surplus national energy. The internal problems, which at the same time will be those of the whole world, will therefore force themselves irresistibly to the front.

The first of all these problems, no one can doubt, is that of bread for all…He ought equally to learn how to develop, not only his muscles, but all the intellectual and moral forces of his being.

…Let the double ideal—bread for the body and bread for the mind—be assured to all, and how many other desirable things would thereby be on the road to accomplishment. One form of progress never comes alone; it presents itself again in other forms of progress throughout the social evolution. The sense of justice being satisfied by the participation of all in the material and intellectual possessions of humanity, there would come to every man a singular lightening of conscience; for the condition of cruel inequality, which overloads some with superfluous wealth while it deprives others of everything, even of hope, weighs as remorse, consciously or unconsciously, on the souls of all, especially of the fortunate, and always mixes a poison with their joys...The moral results of this simple act of justice, the guarantee of food and instruction to all, would be incalculable.

. . . . . .

Under a thousand apparent changes in the surface, the work is being accomplished in the depths of the nations. Thanks to the increasing knowledge men are gaining of themselves and others, they are arriving by degrees at the discovery of the common ground upon which we all resemble each other, and at getting rid of superficial opinions which keep us apart. We are, then, steadily advancing towards future reconciliation, and, by this very fact, towards a form of happiness very different in extent to that which sufficed our forefathers—the animals and the primitive men. Our material and moral world becomes more vast, and this in itself increases our conception of happiness, which henceforward will only be held to be such on condition of its being shared by all; of its being made conscious and rational, and of its embracing in its scope the earnest researches of science and the possessions of art.

It is, then, with all confidence that we reply to the question which every man asks himself: Yes, humanity has really progressed, from crisis to crisis and from relapse to relapse, since the beginning of those millions of years which constitute the short conscious period of our life.

• • • • • •

Archdall Reid

"Characters, Congenital and Acquired" (1897)

Like patriotism, or devotion to a particular religious system, or a knowledge of language, or of letters, or of the uses of steam, or of the bicycle, the altruistic feelings are purely acquired (and not transmissible), and are not immediate products of evolution, but result indirectly from the evolution of man's mental receptivity, that is, from the evolution of his vast power of acquiring mental characters...We need not wait, then, the slow evolution of the social millennium by the accumulation of inborn altruistic variations, as Mr. Kidd expects, nor by the accumulation (and transmission) of acquired variations, as Mr. Spencer expects. Were we all agreed as to the training of our children it would be achievable in the very next generation, for surely, if a generation can be reared to reverence a stick or a stone, an inanimate idol...it can be reared also to love and reverence man.

We hear of the evolution of morals or of language or of religion, of the printing press, of the locomotive, of the bicycle, and so forth. In the popular mind, and, I fear, even in the minds of some scientific men, this evolution ranks as a process of the same order as the evolution of a plant or animal. Evolution means unfolding, and therefore, the word is perhaps correctly applied to the bicycle, etc. But there is this essential difference between a living being and the bicycle: The former is the progeny of a parent; the latter is not. So also the language of to-day is in a figurative sense only the progeny of the language of the former times; the morals of to-day, have, in a figurative sense only, descended from those of yesterday. All these things are human inventions, and belong not to human evolution, but to what has been called evolution in the environment. The so-called 'Social Evolution,' of which we have lately heard so much, is therefore a myth from the biological standpoint. As I have said, and as I wish to iterate and reiterate, neither the altruistic feelings in particular, nor morals in general, nor anything of the kind, has undergone evolution in man. What has undergone evolution is his enormous power of acquiring characters, these among other things.

• • • • • •

Henry Jones
"Social and Individual Evolution" (1898)

We are at last becoming aware of the fact that, side by side, or even continuous with, the natural cosmos, there exists another cosmos, a stable order of human relations which, like the former, has its general uniformities awaiting to be interpreted by means of universal principles. The desire to comprehend the laws of the order of civilized society, and of directing and controlling to some extent the forces that struggle and combine within it, is destined to deepen and to spread. Wherever we turn we find men discussing what are called "social problems." All the great organs of public thought—the pulpit, the platform and the press—are eloquent with this theme. Many of these problems are old, although even these are propounded to us in a new way by our own times: but some of them are the products of conditions that never existed before. All of them alike have become more urgent, for we have become more sensitive to them; so that we cannot avoid them; we cannot even postpone them...It is well for us that, as a rule, the times which set the problem generally contribute something to the solution as well. And if the social problem has in our day become more acute in many important respects than it ever was before, the intellectual and moral conditions under which the answer may be sought have also become more favourable.

. . . . . .

[T]he conditions of practical life in civilized society have changed during the last sixty years in the most fundamental manner. Modern invention has led to the organization of industry, to the stratification of society into classes with common and yet competing professional and commercial interests, and to the establishment of an economic *world* on a most sensitive and unstable equilibrium, — phenomena to which the past offers hardly any parallel. All the familiar landmarks of social economy have been swept away. We are constrained to ask with new seriousness, "What is this social machine which I have helped to create, which reveals to me at the same moment both my weakness and my strength, and which is at once my master and my servant? And what kind of being is he who expresses his nature this way?"

. . . . . .

Society is a hyper-organism. It shows a tendency to be *all* in *every* part, in a way to which the physical organism furnishes no adequate parallel. A society has not reached its ideal until it has as many centres of conscious activity as it has members. To the individual who does not comprehend his relations to his fellows, the community is a mechanical system and a hard taskmaster. He is implicitly at war with it, and a public danger. And a society—be it a family, a municipality, a church or a state—is really *one* only if all that are in it are also of it; only if its meaning is open to all its members and its purposes beat in every one of its organs. The truth of individuality is thus to be found in a fully organized society; and of society in a fully developed individual.

. . . . . .

The evolution of the individual's powers is hindered by the hard necessities of an imperfectly moralized social system, and the evolution of the public good is baffled by the narrow views and the unsocialized wills of individuals.

. . . . . .

When we translate this view of "the concomitance of social and individual evolution" into common words, it seems to mean that, as civilization advances, the functions of society as a unity and the functions of individuals within that society are simultaneously enlarged. For evolution means just this increase of function, this capacity of responding in new ways to the demand of the environment—of doing more things and doing them better. And it may well be asked, How is it possible that society can do more and more for its members and at the same time allow, and even enable, them to do more and more for themselves?

    ...It is tacitly assumed that individual enterprise and liberty on the one hand, and communal action or "state interference," on the other, are antagonistic. Human welfare is held to be best secured by maintaining an equilibrium between them, and equilibrium means the equality of *opposing* forces...Nevertheless, obvious as these conclusions may seem to be, I believe they can be shown to imply a view as to the nature of the relation of society to its members which is not less false in theory than mischievous in practice. This view rests, in fact, upon a mechanical metaphor which is not applicable within the sphere of intelligent life; and it is definitely inconsistent with the conception of the growth of personal intelligence and will through the ideal inclusion of social tendencies, and of the growth of society by fuller self-manifestation in the individual character of its members.

. . . . . .

Impossible as it may at first seem to be, that both society and its members may at the same time enlarge their sphere of activity, history shows us that this has actually been taking place. Indeed, I am not sure that anything else of the highest moment has been taking place. For this more intense integration and fuller articulation of the moral cosmos, this synthesis and analysis at one stroke, this growth of society as an active unit and of its members as free and effective personalities within it, is the very essence of civilization.

. . . . . .

We are passing beyond the stage at which public and private ends can be opposed in this abstract way, and beginning to ask whether there are any legitimate social ends that do not find their goal in the individual, or any legitimate personal ends that are not genuinely social in content. If the ends of society and those of the individual come into collision, it is because both society and the individual are in contradiction with themselves. The conflict arises because either the individual or the society has blundered and sought an illegitimate end, even from its own point of view. A social will that does not justify itself in particular benefits to the individuals who constitute the community must delete itself; and an individual end which is anti-social tends to destroy the individual himself.

. . . . . .

[T]here is no...antagonism...between the ideals of a progressive society and of the citizens who live within it. Social evolution and the evolution of individual character are but two aspects of the same fact.

• • • • • •

William Carey Jones

"The Conditions of a Californian Civilization" (1899)

The characteristic of our age is its intense consciousness. We aim to achieve results. Both ends and processes are consciously reflected upon. Even habit, according to which many of our actions are governed, is but the unconscious following of consciously conceived motives. We live far away from the childhood and youth of the race. The country that preëminently represented the adolescent stage of civilized man was Greece. Her culture came without a conscious aiming at results...

Twenty-odd centuries separate us from that age. An opulent inheritance, which we scarcely know how to handle, has been transmitted to us...We have produced complexities of situation which demand higher intellectual powers than even the Greeks possessed. It is an extraordinary condition of things that mankind has brought about. Individual man is ahead of the race. Conscience and ethics are beyond intellect. While society needs to be controlled by the intellectual powers, the standard of such control, as well as of individual and social action, is set by a moral demand, which is beyond the ability of his intellectual nature to meet. We are all at sea as to how to compass the results we have set before ourselves. We have conquered an imperial domain of industrial activities, of moral ideals, and of intellectual possibilities, and we don't know how to govern it. We have weaved a complex web about ourselves, and we have lost the thread that leads to the masterful position. Labor is divided, diversified, and emancipated, but the laborer is in worse thralldom. Riches are enormously accumulated, and the possibilities of spiritual and material happiness seem attainable, and yet the problem of poverty sets us aghast and helpless. Science has opened the heart of nature and converted her laws and processes to man's service, and yet life has become only more complex, toilsome, and feverish. Learning has become widely diffused, yet rational education is still distant. Democracy is overspreading the world, yet practical and efficient political management is all but lacking.

A higher grade of intelligence is needed...It is a crude thought which says that we have the best we deserve, whether in government, in institutions, in education, in social conditions. We, in fact, deserve far better than we have. The instincts and moral demands of the people are far better than their knowledge of how to satisfy them. Of course, the moral life of individuals and of communities is far from perfect...But this fact does not seriously modify the statement that our moral longings are entirely beyond the competence of our intelligence to meet...It behooves especially all of us who are charged with any part of the guidance of society so to build upon ourselves that each succeeding generation shall approach nearer to the goal of the things worthy of it. The problem of civilization presents itself to each community in the world in much the same way as the problem of culture and character presents itself to the individual man. It is mainly a problem of self-culture. Self-making, in the higher sense, is the condition of a perfected society or of the perfected man.

. . . . . .

We are no longer unconscious, or semi-conscious, adolescents like the Greeks of thirty centuries ago, but adult men with all the burden of responsibility that consciousness and a knowledge of the world's experience give to action. We don't know whether to shirk or to act. If we resolve to act, we don't know in what direction to set our activity. Our half-understood historical knowledge misleads us. At one moment we lay too much stress upon the effects of environment. At another moment we account all progress as owing to man, to individual action, or to the concerted action of communities. Race-tides and world-tides overwhelm us with their force, and we deem ourselves helpless to make our destiny. We are in turn self-conceited in contemplation of our position, physical, social, intellectual, or industrial; and then again abashed by the fear of our neighbors' criticism. It is difficult to walk the *via media* between over-self-confidence and timidity.

. . . . . .

That our modern life is largely institutional and social rather than personal makes the problem of our civilization in appearance perhaps somewhat different from that of other times.

• • • • • •

L.T. Hobhouse
Mind in Evolution (1901)

Of the total growth of mind in scope and power during the existence of the human race, at least one half must be assigned to the comparatively short period from the beginnings of Greek history to the present day. But it must be remembered that the greater part of this period still lies outside the scope of "self-conscious evolution." It is only in modern times, as I hope to show in detail on another occasion, that the threads begin to be drawn together to weave the larger purpose. Up to this point civilisation still moves in large measure through conflict, though the social systems, the principles, the purposes that conflict are wider, and give more scope for internal development. As civilised societies become more highly organised and their ideas more comprehensive, the onward movement in each becomes more sure and its orbit more vast. And yet, to this day, how great a proportion of the energies of the best and ablest men is spent in combating one another. If we can imagine all this energy harmonised by the conception of a great pervading purpose, we can form some conception of the increased efficiency with which "self-conscious evolution" would bring its forces to bear.

. . . . . .

With the mastery of external nature, applied science has made us all familiar. But the last enemy that man shall overcome is himself. The internal conditions of life, the physiological basis of mental activity, the sociological laws that operate for the most part unconsciously, are parts of the "environment" which the self-conscious intelligence has to master, and it is on this mastery that the *regnum hominis* will rest.

• • • • • •

Benjamin Kidd
Principles of Western Civilisation (1902)

The meaning of the evolutionary drama that is working itself out in Western history has been the same from the beginning. It continues to be the same as far as human eye can forecast the future. It is, so far as science is concerned with it, the great drama in which the tyranny of the present is being lifted, for the first time in the world's history, from the shoulders of the human race.

. . . . . .

[I]n the development in progress under our eyes in Western history we are regarding the main sequence of events along which the meaning of the cosmic process in human history is descending towards the future. Transforming as has been the many sided conflict we have followed through the past, it can, therefore, hardly be regarded as more than the prelude to the wider and more conscious phase of the struggle towards which the world is converging.

. . . . . .

We seem to see, as it were, the conscious intellectual process in our civilisation slowly overtaking the meaning of the evolutionary process which, independent of that consciousness, has been taking its way through history in advance of it...The central principle of the evolutionary principle of the evolutionary drama in progress in the world, namely, that it is the meaning of the struggle between the future and the present which controls all the ultimate tendencies of progress, and into which all the phenomena of history are gradually being drawn, has remained, we see, outside the field of Mr. Spencer's vision.

. . . . . .

It may be observed that in considering the recent past of the evolutionary process in the modern world, the outward feature with which we have been principally occupied has been capable of being summed up in the single word— emancipation. The period has been one of the general enfranchisement of all the conditions and forms of human activity. It has been the era of the emancipation of creeds and of commerce, of industry and of thought, of individuals, of classes, and of nationalities.

• • • • • •

Ira W. Howerth
"Education and Social Progress" (1902)

Individual teleology has…been practiced since the dawn of intellect. The instances in which it has been applied to social development, however, are rare. Certain individuals in the past—kings, emperors, statesmen, and the like—have identified their own interests with those of the social group to which they belonged, and have in consequence employed design in their endeavor to achieve a definite social end. In still rarer circumstances individuals have made the welfare of their social group the center of their interests and the object of their endeavors, and, having conceived an ideal destiny for their group, or an ideal humanity, have striven consciously to attain it. Such individuals as are represented by these two classes furnish us the only examples of individuotelic social progress.

When the social group itself becomes conscious of its development, projects an aim, and sets about the intelligent employment of means to realize its aim, the process of development becomes sociotelic. Sociotelic development is exactly parallel to what I have called the autotelic development of the individual. It takes place only when the social group takes its affairs into its own hands, consciously formulates its own purposes, and strives to accomplish them in the same manner as an individual seeks to promote his own welfare. Obviously this is the highest phase of social development, the phase in which there is the highest possibility of organizing and employing socially progressive forces, of which education is potentially the greatest, to avoid friction and eliminate waste. It is to society exactly what the self-conscious phase of his own education is to the individual.

...Now, it must be confessed that modern society is far from having attained the condition here implied. It has barely entered upon the rational stage of social evolution. Here and there may indeed be found vague indications of a social consciousness as manifested in some example of sociotelic action. A democratic form of government, certain instances of legislation, and the social employment of an educational system for promoting social welfare may be cited as initial steps in the sociotelic field. But there is as yet no true democracy, and the legislative and educational factors, tho popularly designed for the advancement of general well-being, are still almost universally employed as a means for conserving or promoting personal or class interests. Social progress has hithero taken place almost entirely under the operation of natural forces, and has consequently illustrated the wastefulness and extravagance observed in the lowest processes of nature. The progress which has been achieved by modifications of the material environment, by legislative enactments, and by systems of education has been usually the unintended result of movements to promote other ends. It has not been the object primarily sought to be attained. Neither education, legislation, nor the subjection of nature can produce the most wholesome effects as factors in social development until they are scientifically ordered by the social consciousness. We are just now entering upon the sociotelic, or socially conscious stage of social evolution, the possibilities of which are almost undreamed of.

• • • • • •

Dennis Hird
An Easy Outline of Evolution (1903)

To fully grasp the teaching of Evolution is to pass from a condition of helpless isolation to one of universal brotherhood with the universe. Man is no longer to be treated as a solitary, maimed lodger in a world of dust and ashes. But by learning the laws of the universe, and by knowing that he, too, must conform to those laws, he is enabled to march unerringly to the highest goal.

• • • • • •

Richard T. Ely
Studies in the Evolution of Industrial Society (1903)

To an ever-increasing extent, as so frequently stated, society is governed by the operation of self-conscious social forces. There is a dawning self-consciousness of society, and there is clear evidence of a determination on the part of society that the advantages of civilization shall be widely diffused.

• • • • • •

George F. Wilkin
Control in Evolution (1903)

The controlling principle of evolution at the present time is the rational will of man. What gravitation once was for a certain stage of evolution; what chemical affinity was for a later and higher stage; what life was for a still more advanced period; that the practical reason of man now is—the supreme controlling principle of the world.

. . . . . .

So soon as reason became self-conscious in man, and master of itself, it refused to acknowledge any man as master, in any capacity in life, save by its own election. When that point was reached, and not till then, Manhood became conscious of itself...And then, for the first time in history, a *rational* sociology became possible. For, until then, society itself had been in leading strings. Not yet having attained to the prerogative of rational self-determination, it was not prepared to understand, much less to formulate, the principles of a social order and a social progress based upon rational self-determination. Science is an interpretation of fact, not a formulation of prophetic speculation; and thus society's actual attainment of her maturity must antedate the scientific formulation of a doctrine of society's maturity.

. . . . . .

All that is needed to make this conception a thoroughly working reality, is a very little further development of the average American citizen in the intelligent grasp of public interests, in independent self-determination toward evolutionary ends, and in facility in the invention and manipulation of machinery for the expression of public opinion.

. . . . . .

Our ultimate conception of society supposes...the active cooperation of *all men* in the maintenance and promotion of all human interests; and it looks forward to a time, in the evolutionary movement of society, when national boundaries, interests, and sympathies, will be seen to have but a subsidiary function as stepping-stones to the unification and complete civilization of Humanity.

. . . . . .

The great difficulties of social evolution do not arise from the normal resistance of a lower to the introduction of a higher order of existence; but from an abnormal resistance—a resistance due to *anti-evolutionary self-determinations by the supreme controlling principle—the rational will—itself.* I have already adverted to the fact that many men, who know the true life and their duty to live it, yet choose the base life of animal self-indulgence—a life that is not merely *not* evolutionary, and not merely *resistant* to evolution; but it is a life that involves all the power of human nature in a more or less direct and consciously coherent *effort to subvert evolution.* In other words...the base and anti-evolutionary choices that men make and have made, result in an evolution of humanity downward—a movement fitly characterized as a *counter*-evolution.

. . . . . .

That cosmic evolution—a process extending over millions of years and comprehending the sum total of all that falls within the range of human cognition; a process characterized in the past by movement so stupendous as utterly to baffle human thought:—that cosmic evolution should come at last to depend upon the directive wisdom of the human mind and upon the propelling energy of the human will, and should nevertheless still retain its character as *cosmic* evolution:—is a conception so astounding, so foreign to the experience of any single human being, that, although philosophy, science, and religion unite to pronounce it true, it would not be strange if the human intellect should halt, perplexed and sometimes paralyzed, before the contemplation, especially in some of its practical aspects.

• • • • • •

John Dewey
"Democracy in Education" (1903)

Modern life means democracy, democracy means freeing intelligence for independent effectiveness—the emancipation of mind as an individual organ to do its own work. We naturally associate democracy, to be sure, with freedom of action, but freedom of action without freed capacity of thought behind it is only chaos...How does the school stand with reference to this matter?...[T]he school has lagged behind the general contemporary social movement; and much that is unsatisfactory, much of conflict and of defect, comes from the discrepancy between the relatively undemocratic organization of the school, as it affects the mind of both teacher and pupil, and the growth and extension of the democratic principle in life beyond school doors.

. . . . . .

The forces of social life are already encroaching upon the school institutions which we have inherited from the past, so that many of its main stays are crumbling. Unless the outcome is to be chaotic, we must take hold of the organic, positive principle involved in democracy, and put that in entire possession of the spirit and work of the school.

● ● ● ● ● ●

J. Paul Goode
"The Human Response to the Physical Environment"
(1904)

Human development, physical and social, is, at the start, unconscious, a direct response to the conditions of the physical environment—a cosmic process. But the psychic, social element enters, and the experience of the race is gradually capitalized in the form of social institutions and conventions. These become forces competent to shape further progress, but they are clearly secondary, depending for initiation and for direction upon the conditions of the physical environment. Progress in social evolution is a record of the changing ratio between the influence of the physical environment and this growing social environment. This changing ratio shows a growing independence of the physical environment on the part of man, even a domination over it. It may be represented graphically by a parallelogram, the length of which, AB, stands for the lapse of ages occupied by human evolution, and this may be four or five million years, if we may dare try to convert geological ages to years.

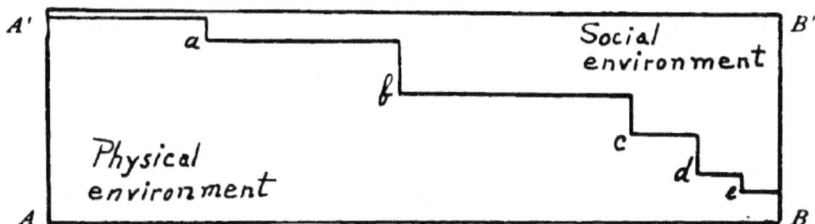

The vertical ordinates *AA'*, *BB'*, represent in the terminal epochs the sum total of the forces in our environment, both physical and social, and may be most easily thought of in percentage, up to 100, at the top line. With the *homo alalus* the social environment was at a minimum, almost zero; the physical environment essentially 100 per cent. On the invention of language (*a*) a sudden access of social power makes a large conquest over the physical control. With the discovery of fire (*b*) another conquest over nature changes the ratio, reducing the control of the physical environment. Agriculture (*c*), domestication of beasts of burden (*d*), and every useful discovery or invention, mechanical or social, have changed the ratio, giving us added dominion over the elements of our physical environment. But we can never reduce this environment to zero. Be we never so wise and ingenious, we shall always be directed, and in the course of our evolution will be conditioned by its elements. These forces may be unseen, but they are nevertheless potent, and they are eternal.

• • • • • •

Edgar A. Ashcroft
The World's Desires (1905)

Men can now, for the first time in human history, perceive the important truth that the personal activities of humanity *can*...be so ordered as, in all reasonable probability, to produce a continual progress, uniformly accelerating, in place of the erratic and intermittent waves of advance and retrogression by which, hithero, humanity in common with all unintelligent nature, has proceeded.

. . . . . .

[M]ankind is reaching out towards something better, is on the ascending line on the curve of evolution, is *changing* its very nature.

● ● ● ● ● ●

Ernest Untermann
Science and Revolution (1905)

Conscious human co-operation in the struggle against nature merely inaugurates a new cycle of cosmic evolution. This cycle cannot end in the abolition of the universal struggle, because the universe, being infinite, always generates the elements for new negations. Yet each new negation henceforth implies the improved co-operation of human beings in the control of evolutionary processes.

. . . . . .

An evolutionary ethic demands the abolition of all economic, political, and intellectual oppression; a reduction in the struggle for the material requirements of life to a minimum by collective control of productive processes; an understanding of cosmic, social, and individual evolution;

sexual selection of evolutionary cultures; and a control of self in accord with the requirements of universal evolution through the fulfillment of the preceding conditions.

• • • • • •

J. Lionel Tayler
"Aspects of Individual Evolution" (1906)

The *distinctively human* applications of a great principle are generally perceived long after its first enunciation. For the vast stretches of thought that are opened up by any new conception of the universe perplex the mind and give it a temporary feeling of desolation and loneliness. It is only when the changed outlook has become familiar, only when the most prominent features of the new horizon have been localised, when the whole country has been explored and a rough survey been made, that the mind can then turn its attention from the *general* changes that have taken place to those that are *particular* and *personal*, to discover that here also things that are vital to its very existence are altered and can no longer be thought of in the old way. So men and women, awed by the vastness of the evolutionary theory, have studied deeply geological, astronomical, and general biological facts, but have as yet left untouched the one transcendent problem—the study of the development of their own individual existence.

. . . . . .

That some sort of development does take place will be, readily granted; for the stages of infancy, childhood, adolescence, and maturity are too well recognised and too firmly established to admit denial; but it is doubtful if these periods are ever interpreted in evolutionary terms. They are, to most of us, merely phases in a general growth instead of being new possibilities for the realization of a larger and a more progressive life.

...[I]f there be a steady evolution of character after birth, if this be, as it must be if it exist at all, as much a needed unfolding of life-powers and as vital to the formation of healthy adult character as the regular unfolding of the pre-natal stages are to the formation of healthy infancy, surely it must be a matter of grave concern to all who are interested in the welfare of humanity to see that each child shall have a chance of reaching his or her adult stage of existence unharmed by harmful interference.

. . . . . .

It is ignorance, and ignorance only, of the vast complexities of development that make the teacher and the parent so ready to force their own ideas and methods of living on those of the child. Could they but realise even vaguely the unbroken series of changes that grow more complex in character and not less as embryonic life is left behind, they would understand the folly of attempting with this crude modeller's knowledge to fashion something that requires the knowledge of a God.

. . . . . .

It is obvious that the subject of individual evolution could never have been pursued either as a study or as a practical life-aim except in civilised and more or less protected surroundings. For the uncertainties of primitive existence must always have kept primitive man in such a state of alertness against possible foes that he would have had neither times nor inclination for thought, nor even for premeditated action. Beyond, therefore, the growth of certain customs, in relation to shelter, food and parentage, savage life affords little that can be thought of as in any way related to this, the most modern of all modern sciences.

Neither can much that is of practical value be obtained from a study of ancient civilisations, for not only do we know little beyond the barest outline of the inner lives of the citizens of these states, so that their individual daily habits and customs are to us a matter of probable or improbable conjecture and no more, and their life-lore, if they had any, is therefore unknown to us, but the fact no old-world philosophy recognised the principle of progressive growth, made it impossible even for such an enlightened people as the Greeks to realise the thought of an ordered life-chain reaching forward, stage by stage, from the very beginning to the very end of existence.

...Briefly, then, this study is modern. It is concerned with the development of the whole individual during the whole course of his or her existence; and since its teachings can only be fostered and made practical within the limits of a progressive state that is itself a leader among other civilised states, it is clear that this individual study must be bounded by the limits of a just social horizon. Looking, therefore, at our subject from the individual point of view, we shall yet have to remember that it is socially environed.

Such is the boundary of a kingdom that is more exclusively man's own than any other that he is in possession of, and it has a beauty and richness that is his alone; and yet, with his characteristic backwardness to utilise that which is near at hand and search for opportunities that are far away, he has passed by this kingdom and left it, so that it remains unexplored and tractless.

. . . . . .

The evolutionist is no believer in sudden transitions. He finds wherever he looks definite evidence of slow but ordered change; he expects, therefore, that character, in its development, will conform to this general fact. He sees, if he is observant, that the growth capacity of even the lower type of child is stupendous—that it begins life healthily—and he sees with pain a process antagonistic to natural growth set in as a result of debased surroundings...He notes...girls and boys growing older stage by stage, *but not progressing*, neither gaining in sensitiveness nor strength of feeling, nor in wisdom and strength of will for the added years that have come to them...He sees the desire to know—a priceless endowment of humanity—warped by careless training, till when adolescence is reached it has become simply an unwholesome and prurient curiosity; and again he is compelled to realise how often this distorted adolescence leads through a wrongly chosen calling and a mercenary or brutal marriage, with wasted life-aim and soiled and evil parentage, to a gross materialistic middle period of life that is not mature but simply barbaric, in which the barbarian prides himself on his barbarism, and is gratified by the fact that he has "outgrown his childhood's ideals," and, having lost what is human, is satisfied with what is merely animal, till at the last this withered adult totters to the grave obstinately adhering to his twisted and distorted past.

For the man or woman who foregoes his or her youthful life-aims there is no morrow, for the purpose of existence is destroyed.

Some people who have had experience, but whose own life has not been distorted to the extent that most others have, say this destruction of natural girlish and boyish hopes is a small matter. "What if children are cramped at home by uncongenial surroundings? what if a woman's ideals are somewhat soiled after marriage, and she comes to experience what is material and lose the ideal? what if a man is turned into an automaton by work that mars his powers? Well! The woman adjusts herself, and so does the man, and they don't appear to be very unhappy as the result of it." This is not the evolutionist's view.

To him this distortion of character, this violation of an individual's rights, this violation of a nation's life, by destroying the efficiency of its several citizens, is the most tragic fact that the world knows of. A tragedy that is epic in its supreme awfulness, and he feels that these things should not and shall not be.

. . . . . .

The evolutionist does not believe in the meanness of existence, for he knows something of the great forces that have moved forward age by age, and he would teach the child to catch something of this forward spirit also. He would make it feel the true greatness of its own existence, the wonder of its beginning, the wonder of its birth, the glory of its own evolution. He would try to make the child *feel* the drift of its own being towards adolescence and to trust the mind promotings that a healthy adolescence brings. He would teach the maiden or lad to prepare for the responsibilities of adult life and adults to live cleanly in the thought of what is before them, in the belief that uncontrolled low life and low actions soil and dishonour what is high, and he would try to show even though it be in merest outline the beauty of human life-love, of the individualized home, of wife, husband and child; the fineness of any trade or any profession that is taken up because, and only because, of the distinctive individual interest that it has aroused in the man or woman who would make it a calling. These things he would teach so that the individual, living constantly in the shadow and hope of the future and guided by the experience of the past with its long upward course, will come to realise that life is pregnant with its own religion and feeling, and the tendencies which it discloses are both purposeful and great. To such a person, so developed, the endeavour to practically realise the *individual* human life-aim will seem the obvious but not common-place object for which we all live.

• • • • • •

Gaylord Wilshire
Wilshire Editorials (1906)

As man becomes more and more conscious of the relation he bears to human society in particular and the universe in general he increases his capacity of life. *The greatest capacity for life would exist in a man developed to the highest degree spiritually, mentally and physically, and living in a self-conscious society having the most perfect command of and knowledge of itself and of its own relation to the universe.*

• • • • • •

Thomas Davidson
A History of Education (1907)

We can now clearly see, and all true educators do see, that education is conscious evolution of the entire human being through ever closer relations, intellectual, affectional and ethical, to the entire universe, human and subhuman. The only question that remains is: How can these relations be most readily and most securely established? Even this question is already partly answered, and will be more fully answered in the future.

• • • • • • •

Editorial, Quarterly Newsbook of the Municipal University, Kansas City (1907)

Our system of education is…the germ of a new order. It contains within itself all the organs, the institutions of a society that shall be at once conceptive and capable— fulfilling high designs. The broadest and plainest fact about the history of society hithero is its disappointment, its recurrent dead-lock and self-destruction. There is an important sense in which one may say that social progress has not yet fairly begun. *There has been no real and important social progress hithero—only a slow movement through the difficult lessons of disaster toward those grounds of social health upon which for the first time it shall be possible to make gains that cannot be lost.* The story of human experience has not yet reached the date of the beginning of true evolutionary society…We have not yet arrived upon the firm ground of nature and cosmic evolutionary law. But we should take heart, for we have made all the stages of a mighty spiritual pilgrimage from Stygian darkness and confusion of will to the frontiers of a fair land of art and science—the gates of an imperishable civilization.

• • • • • •

Maurice Maeterlinck
"Our Social Duty" (1907)

[H]umanity, we are told, has for more than a century been passing through the most fruitful and victorious, probably the climacteric years of its destiny. It seems, if we consider its past, to be in the decisive phase of its evolution. One would think, from certain indications, that it is nigh upon attaining its apogee. It is traversing a period of inspiration wherewith none other is historically to be compared. A trifle, a last effort, a flash of light which shall connect or emphasise the discoveries, the intuitions scattered or held in suspense alone separates it, perhaps, from the great mysteries. It has lately touched upon problems whose solution, at the cost of the hereditary enemy, that is of the great unknown phenomenon of the universe, would probably render useless all the sacrifices which justice demands of men. Is it not dangerous to stop this flight, to disturb this precious, precarious and supreme minute? Admitting even that what is gained can no longer be lost, as in the earlier upheavals, it is nevertheless to be feared lest the vast disorganisation required by equity should put an abrupt end to this happy period; and it is not sure but that its reappearance might be long delayed, the laws which preside over the inspiration of the genius of the race being as capricious, as unstable as those which preside over the inspiration of the genius of the individual.

. . . . . .

Can we foresee what will happen when the human race as a whole will be taking part in the intellectual labour which is the labour proper to our species? To-day, hardly one brain in ten thousand exists in conditions entirely favourable to its activity. There is, at this moment, a monstrous waste of spiritual force. Idleness at the top depresses as many mental energies as excess of manual labour annihilates below. It is incontestable that, when it shall be given to all men to apply themselves to the task at present reserved for a few favourites of chance, humanity will increase a thousandfold its prospects of attaining the great mysterious aim.

. . . . . .

Let us think sometimes of the great invisible ship that carries our human destinies upon eternity. Like the vessels of our confined oceans, she has her sails and her ballast. The fear that she may pitch or roll on leaving the roadstead is no reason for increasing the weight of the ballast by stowing the fair, white sails in the depths of the hold. They were not woven to moulder side by side with cobble-stones in the dark. Ballast exists everywhere: all the pebbles of the harbour, all the sand on the beach will serve for it. But sails are rare and precious things: their place is not in the murk of the well, but amid the light of the tall masts, where they will collect the winds of space.

● ● ● ● ● ●

James Thompson Bixby
The Ethics of Evolution (1907)

In the light of modern science, humanity is one vast organism, whose span of life runs back to the very dawn of animal existence upon the earth. We who are now on the stage are not only the inheritors of the past, but the living embodiments and trustees of the life of the future. By our unfaithfulness and negligence we can retard and mar the progress of humanity; by our diligence and loyalty we preserve and further it. As the child is father to the man, as the habits, efforts, and even ideals of the youth still live within the statesman and the philosopher, so the thoughts and deeds of our ancestors live in the spiritual life of to-day, and ours shall live in the victories or disappointments of posterity. We have no more a right than we have a possibility of living to ourselves alone, or for the present, independent of the past and the future.

. . . . . .

We are bound therefore, in our moral decisions, to recognize these universal relations of every meanest individual. We are bound to weigh our actions and motives with regard to their influence on the elevation or depression of the human race as a whole. The great law of duty is to make, not one cell or nerve of the body politic flourish, but the great all connected whole of social life progress to higher life, rational, emotional, moral, and spiritual.

The ultimate standard, then, for determining what is morally good and morally bad is its tendency to help forward or impede this progress of our race toward the ideal of humanity. The supreme end of moral action is the evolution of the completest and highest soul-life of humanity...Those motives are morally bad which tend to lower, impede, or degrade this spiritual development.

• • • • • •

Robert Gunn Davis
"Some Tendencies in Social Evolution" (1908)

The age we live in has become disgracefully artificial, and it is largely the pronounced character of this artificiality which has accentuated, if not largely created, the evils of modern civilization...The artificiality of life which comes of material advancement without any restraint, is the one great obstacle to the rational development of society. Happily, there is reason to believe that the movements which are progressing among the civilized peoples, bid fair to herald the dawn of a day of greater wisdom than has yet been known, for greater efforts than hithero are being made to discount the advantages of phenomenal material prosperity.

Three distinct movements, which are advancing simultaneously, give some assurance of the progress of mankind towards a higher state of life than the world has yet known; (1) the movement towards freedom and clearness in thinking; (2) the movement towards simplicity of life; and (3) the movement which has for its object the improvement of the social environment. The first of these great movements has been long in gaining strength, but at last there are signs that masses of the people have learned the advantage of the unrestricted use of the mental faculties, and have come to recognise the important part which complete freedom in thinking plays in the progress of everything which makes for the advancement of Man. The movement towards simplicity of life is, however, but meagrely understood yet...The movement towards the improvement of the social environment has, however, in the past few years, made enormous progress, and its progress is one of the most encouraging signs of the humanist tendencies of modern times. While much remains to be done by the individual, which might well be done, it is a happy augury for the future that a consciousness of the general unsatisfactoriness of social conditions is being developed among all classes.

. . . . . .

The present is a time of almost unprecedented political and social optimism in this country, and this is why it is wise to look at the dangers ahead…Never until it can be shown to the people that the influences which enslave them to-day are mental, physical, and social, rather than political evils, will definite and lasting progress be recorded.

• • • • • •

Ira W. Howerth
"The Social Ideal" (1908)

If, by taking thought, we could project a social ideal upon which the people could agree, one which, because drawn from facts and existing conditions, and the possibilities of human nature, would force its acceptance on every reflective mind, we should have the most effective means of increasing the rapidity of human advancement. Such an ideal would stimulate enthusiasm, promote progressive efforts and unify them by a community of purpose. It would clear away numerous logical barriers in social thought, and straighten the zigzag path of progress…So far are we, however, from any agreement as to what society ought to be that we have not seriously turned our attention to the subject.

. . . . . .

The construction or projection of a social ideal is not, as some seem to suppose, a matter of foreseeing the course of the unconscious evolution of society. Social phenomena are so complex that social prophecies are likely to be abortive...[A] social ideal differs from a social forecast. It is a conception of what society ought to be, not of what it is to become. It is ethical. It implies the categorical imperative. It must, therefore, be a work of synthesis, or, if you please, a product of the constructive imagination.

The ideals of society hitherto constructed, and with which men have been most familiar, have been, of course, too largely works of the imagination—the Utopias of Plato, More, Bellamy and the like. They lacked foundation in fact. They were not in harmony with human aspirations, desires and frailties...What we need now, however, and what with our wider knowledge we ought to be able approximately to construct, is an ideal scientifically conceived, in harmony with existing facts and forces, and hence possible of attainment...Such an ideal would not be separable and distinct from society as we now find it, but its highest manifestation—society purified and transformed by the best elements it now contains...All that social philosophy should now undertake is to determine the main features of an ultimate social ideal. It cannot describe the daily life of the citizen of an ideal world, but it can answer the questions: Is the coming society to be based on the class spirit or on the spirit of brotherhood? Is it to be competitive or cooperative? Individualistic or socialistic?

. . . . . .

Intelligent men do not necessarily guarantee an intelligent society. Social imbecility is not infrequent manifested by an intelligent community...We Americans are a "free and intelligent people," and yet we sometimes allow ourselves to be represented in the municipal council, in the legislature or in the Congress by men who do not represent even the average intelligence of the community. We allow the management of public utilities to rest in the hands of those who control them for their own individual profit. We allow cesspools to form in the slums of our cities, where poverty, disease and crime are generated, where human beings are huddled together like so many animals, and who in their brutish environment naturally tend to become "dumb, driven cattle." We are more or less indifferent to the premature exhaustion of our natural resources by greedy corporations, and can witness without manifest alarm the sacrifice of future to present prosperity by the over-employment of women and children.

. . . . . .

Socially we are far from brilliant...Until the people are socially well informed...there will be no high manifestation of social intelligence...This ideal intelligence of society involves no new creation, no importation of an imaginary element. Some social intelligence now exists...[It] began to manifest itself without the conscious employment of means and methods of developing it...But the formation of social intelligence is artificial as well as natural. Having arrived at a stage of development at which we realize the importance of a corporate consciousness, we have already begun to devise methods of promoting it...When it is generally recognized and accepted that social intelligence is the fundamental element in the social ideal for which all should strive, a conscious use of all available means for promoting it will follow.

. . . . . .

As social intelligence advances, social economy increases; when the former becomes ideal, so does the latter. Social intelligence, then, as well as social economy, demand thorough social or democratic organization for supplying social needs. Such organization must, therefore, be progressively realized as intelligence and economy approach perfection. Democracy is the ultimate form of government. It is not "an experiment which may be abandoned, but an evolution which must be fulfilled."

. . . . . .

We have now shown that the social ideal is represented by the conception of a society with a perfectly developed corporate consciousness, democratically organized on the basis of social economy, and having its members inspired by the spirit of conscious and voluntary cooperation for the public good. It is a cooperative commonwealth in which the good of each, while subordinate to, is yet realized in, the good of all.

. . . . . .

[O]f what value is this ideal in respect to the current questions of the day?...The end suggests the means. All things must be made to work together for the attainment of the preconceived end. The ideal, if we would but admit it, is the most practical thing in the world…The social ideal we have suggested is attainable, for it demands only the completion of existing elements in society. As to its loftiness and worth, we have only to reflect upon what its approximate realization would necessarily mean. It would mean a society…which in truth will mean a new heaven and a new earth where man, untrammeled by want and evil conditions, may press rapidly onward in his development and mount to the utmost possibilities of his being.

● ● ● ● ● ●

Leslie Willis Sprague
"The Ethical Reorganization of the Social Ideal" (1909)

Ideals, arising as they do out of human reactions upon economic and social conditions, may be unfolded, unified, made concrete and potent, through the conscious effort of man's reason and conscience. It is here that the task of conscious social evolution should begin. Too long has man been governed by the blind, arbitrary, and slow working processes of nature. At last, as he is learning to understand the evolutionary process, he is permitted to co-operate with nature and accelerate the working of nature's laws, and guard against the unconscionable waste of these arbitrary laws. The social ideal has hitherto been and still is primarily a mere instinctive reaction of man upon his environment. But the social ideal may be made conscious, and by man's effort be clarified and enriched, so as to more adequately inspire and guide him.

. . . . . .

We have not so much a social ideal, as a number of different and often antagonistic social ideals, in American life at the present time. And men are divided by their ideals quite as much as by their personal interests and class and race prejudices…It becomes those who hold to one or another of the various elements of the social ideal, to strive to see the validity of other elements which fellow citizens cherish…The real value of one particular ideal is not known until it is seen in the light of the truth in other partial ideals.

. . . . . .

Society should be so constituted as to afford every individual the fullest and freest opportunity for the development of his or her unique life, in right and helpful relation with others who should be alike free and furthered; a society in which the strong should bear the burden of the weak, to the end that the weak should also become strong; a society in which progress in outward forms should accompany the growing needs of human beings.

. . . . . .

Society has progressed along industrial, scientific and educational lines so rapidly that there has been little energy to give to the moral advancement of mankind...Will it pay? not Is it right? Is the common question to-day.

. . . . . .

The spectacle of poverty...appeals to sympathy and pity...and not as it should to the conscience of mankind. The worse fact is not...that men and women are cold and hungry and wretched in body, but rather that through such conditions they are degraded, the light within them darkened, their minds stunted and deformed, their very souls poisoned by the ignominy they suffer. The saddest fact is not that nerves are hurt, but that the human spirit is injured.

. . . . . .

That which most retards the reorganization of the social ideal, and the realization of the promise which such an ideal would give, is the partial emphasis and narrow interests of different social classes, even reform parties and sects, as well as the stolid indifference of many men and women to any ideal, and the not uncommon lack of moral vision and impulse on the part of even some who consider themselves to be reformers. A broad and inclusive vision, a deep and fervent moral life—these are the needs of our time.

• • • • • •

Charles Horton Cooley
Social Organization (1909)

That which most inwardly distinguishes modern life from ancient or mediaeval is the conscious power of the common people trying to effectuate their instincts. All systems rest, in a sense, upon public opinion; but the peculiarity of our time is that this opinion is more and more rational and self-determining. It is not, as in the past, a mere reflection of conditions believed to be inevitable, but seeks principles, finds these principles in human nature, and is determined to conform life to them or know why not. In this all earnest people, in their diverse ways, are taking part.

. . . . . .

We live in a system and to achieve right ends, or any rational ends whatever, we must learn to understand that system. The public mind must emerge somewhat from its subconscious condition and know and guide its own processes.

• • • • • •

David Staars
The English Woman (1909)

[T]he evolution of humanity implies the necessity of the inner evolution of each individual; consequently general laws must be individually applied, and should determine every conscious effort directed by the individual to his own psychic progress. Henceforth Science is no useless abstraction. It becomes a force capable of influencing every man, pointing a way in which he may labour for his own evolution—that is, his happiness.

Contemporary science seems to be increasingly permeated by this idea. Its scope in the present day is extended in new directions, such as Social Hygiene, Psychology, Mental treatments, Pedagogy. All aim, more or less definitely, at the means of quickening psychic evolution, and some at its application to the individual.

. . . . . .

Seeing that the material and moral progress of humanity depends ultimately upon the psychic evolution of individuals, it is of supreme importance to the future of man that he should possess the means necessary to realise his ideal. But in the present state of society what tools can be used? Commercial undertakings, such as newspapers and other cheap publications, have a certain influence on the masses. But would it be reasonable to expect them to serve this cause efficaciously? From this point of view the study of the woman movement in England seems to be of significance.

• • • • • •

Alice Ravenhill
Quoted in *Euthenics: The Science of Controllable Environment*
(1910)

Quite slowly but surely, the idea is dawning on the social horizon that the persistence of conditions prejudicial to human prosperity is discreditable to a civilized community, and that economics if not ethics calls for their control.

• • • • • •

John S. Welch
Literature in the School (1910)

When we reflect that the teachers in the public schools of this country number more than half a million, that the children between the ages of five and eighteen who attend school number more than twenty-two millions…[w]e must also ask ourselves whether it is possible for this great body of teachers to work with and upon such a large percentage of the entire population, during the impressionable age of childhood, and yet have no influence in shaping the future society which these pupils are to form and in transforming the society which they now do form. Is it reasonable to assume that this money is expended, that these teachers are employed, that these children are accommodated by those who now constitute the state in order that the accumulated treasures of the ages may be preserved and the ideals of the race finally be realized? It is true that the school reflects the ideals of society. It is also true that the school in no small way shapes and modifies the conscious ideals of society. In a more fundamental way the teacher shapes the future because one function of the school is to cause the individual student to set up and to aspire toward worthy ideals, and in the aggregate of individual ideals the social ideal is formed. The social ideal can only be concreted in the ideal of the individual.

Schools exist because the children of men are distinctive among the products of creative energy. They are unique because they can set up and consciously and purposefully aspire toward a definite end or ideal.

• • • • • •

James Harvey Robinson
"The New History" (1911)

History in its broadest sense…is nothing less than the experiences of our race…And what uses are we to make of the experiences of the race? The same kind of use that we make of our own individual history. We may question it, as we question our memory of our personal acts, situations and past ideals…Just as our individual history is thus not immutable but owes its value to its adaptability, so with the history of mankind…History is…not fixed and reducible to outlines and formulas but it is ever alive and ever changing, and it will, if we will but permit it, illuminate and explain our lives as nothing else can do. For our lives, are made up almost altogether of the past and each age should be free to select from the annals of the past those matters which have a bearing on the matters it has specially at heart.

. . . . . .

The ideal history for each of us would be those facts of past human experience to which we should have recourse oftenest to our endeavors to understand ourselves and our fellows. No one account would meet the needs of all, but all would agree that much of what now passes for the elements of history meet the needs of none.

. . . . . .

Obviously history must be rewritten, or rather, innumerable current issues must be given their neglected historic background. Our present so-called histories do not ordinarily answer the questions we would naturally and insistently put to them. When we contemplate the strong demand that women are making for the right to vote, we ask ourselves how did the men win the vote? The historians we consult have scarcely asked themselves that question and so do not answer it. We ask how did our courts come to control legislation in the exceptional and extraordinary manner they do? We look in vain in most histories for a reply. No one questions the inalienable right of the historian to interest himself in any phase of the past that he chooses. It is only to be wished that a greater number of historians had greater skill in hitting upon those phases of the past which serve us best in understanding the most vital problems of the present.

• • • • • •

James Harvey Robinson
The New History (1912)

Previously [history] had been a branch of literature with distinctly literary aims,—when it was not suborned in the interest of theological theories or called upon to stimulate patriotic pride and emulation. But about sixty years ago a new era in historical investigation opened which has witnessed achievements of a character to justify in a measure the complacency in which historians now and then indulge. The most obvious of these achievements seem to me to be four in number, and the historian owes all of them, if I am not mistaken, to the example and influence of natural science. He undertook in the first place to test and examine his sources of information far more critically than ever before, and rejected partially or wholly many authorities upon which his predecessors had relied implicitly. Secondly, he resolved to tell the truth like a man, regardless of whose feelings it might hurt...Thirdly, he began to realize the overwhelming importance of the inconspicuous, the common, and often obscure elements in the past; the homely, every-day, and normal as over against the rare, spectacular, and romantic which had engaged the attention of most earlier writers. Fourthly, he began to spurn supernatural, theological, and anthropocentric explanations which had been the stock-in-trade of the philosophers of history.

. . . . . .

To-day, [the historian] has obviously not only to adjust himself as fast as he can to these new elements in the general intellectual situation, but he must decide what shall be his attitude toward a considerable number of newer sciences of man which, by freely applying the evolutionary theory, have progressed marvelously and are now in a position to rectify many of the commonly accepted conclusions of the historian and to disabuse his mind of many ancient misapprehensions. By the newer sciences of man I mean, first and foremost, anthropology, in a comprehensive sense, prehistoric archeology, social and animal psychology, and the comparative study of religions...These newer social sciences, each studying man in its own particular way, have entirely changed the meaning of many terms which the historian has been accustomed to use in senses now discredited—such words as "race," "religion," "progress," "the ancients," "culture," "human nature," etc. They have vitiated many of the cherished conclusions of mere historians and have served to explain historical phenomena which the historian could by no possibility have rightly interpreted with the means at his disposal.

. . . . . .

In order to understand the light which the discovery of the vast age of mankind casts on our present position, our relation to the past and our hopes for the future, let us borrow, with some modifications, an ingenious device for illustrating modern historical perspective. Let us imagine the whole history of mankind crowded into twelve hours, and that we are living at noon of the long human day. Let us, in the interest of moderation and convenient reckoning, assume that man has been upright and engaged in seeking out inventions for only two hundred and forty thousand years. Each hour on our clock will then represent twenty thousand years, each minute three hundred and thirty-three and a third years. For over eleven and a half hours nothing was recorded. We know of no persons or events; we only infer that man was living on the earth, for we find his stone tools, bits of his pottery, and some of his pictures of mammoths and bison. Not until twenty minutes before twelve do the earliest vestiges of Egyptian and Babylonian civilization begin to appear. The Greek literature, philosophy, and science of which we have been accustomed to speak as "ancient," are not seven minutes old. At one minute before twelve Lord Bacon wrote his Advancement of Learning...and not half a minute has elapsed since man first began to make the steam engine do his work for him. There is, I think, nothing delusive about this reduced scale of things. It is much easier for us to handle and speculate upon than the life-sized picture, which so transcends our experience that we cannot grasp it. *Note: Robinson attributed the above clock metaphor to Heinrich Schmidt.*

. . . . . .

The nineteenth century proved conclusively that [man] *had* been learning and *had* been bettering himself for hundreds of thousands of years. But all this earlier progress had been *unconscious*. For the first time, close upon our own day, progress became an ideal consciously proclaimed and sought. So, whatever the progress of man has been during the twelve hours which we assign to him since he became man, it was only at about one minute to twelve *that he came to wish to progress, and still more recently that he came to see that he can voluntarily progress, and that he has progressed.* This appears to me to be the most impressive message that history has to give us, and the most vital in the light that it casts on the conduct of life.

. . . . . .

If it be conceded that what we rather vaguely and provisionally call social betterment is coming to be regarded by large numbers of thoughtful persons as the chief interest in this game of life, does not the supreme value of history lie for us to-day in the suggestions that it may give us of what may be called the technique of progress, and ought not those phases of the past especially to engross our attention which bear on this essential point?

. . . . . .

The conservative is a perfectly explicable and inevitable product of that long, long period before man woke up to the possibility of conscious betterment. He still justifies existing conditions and ideas by the standards of the past rather than by those of the present or future. He neither vividly realizes how mightily things have advanced in times gone by, nor has he the imagination to see how easily they could be indefinitely bettered, if the temperament which he represents could cease to be artificially fostered...Until very recently the leaders of men have looked backward for their standards and ideals. The intellectual ancestors of the conservative extend back in an unbroken line to the very beginning of human history. The reformer who appeals to the future is a recent upstart. He belongs to the last half minute of our historical reckoning. His family is a new one...But it is clear enough today that the conscious reformer who appeals to the future is the final product of a progressive order of things...We are only just coming to realize that we can coöperate with and direct [the] innate force of change which has so long been silently operating, in spite of the respectable lethargy, indifference, and even protests of man himself, the most educable of all its creatures.

. . . . . .

We make no consistent effort to cultivate a progressive spirit in our boys and girls. They are not made to realize the responsibility that rests upon them—the exhilaration that comes from ever looking and pressing forward. They are still so largely nurtured upon the abstract and the classical that we scarcely yet dare to bring education in relation to life...They are reared with too much respect for the past, too little confidence for the future. Does not education become in this way a mighty barrier cast across the way of progress, rather than a guidepost to betterment?...What would happen if the teachers in our schools and colleges, our theological seminaries and law schools, should make it their business to emphasize the temporary and provisional character of the instruction that they offer, and urge the students to transcend it as fast as a progressive world permitted? The humorous nature of such a suggestion shows how far we are still from any general realization and acceptance of the great lesson of history.

• • • • • •

Morrison I. Swift
Changing the Prisons into Social Schools (1912)

House No. 1247
Bill accompanying the petition of Morrison I. Swift for legislation to change the prisons into social schools.

The Commonwealth of Massachusetts

AN ACT
Changing the Prisons into Social Schools.

Be it enacted by the Senate and the House of Representatives in General Court assembled, and by the authority of the same, as follows:

Section 1.   The prisons of Massachusetts shall be evolved into social schools. They shall combine productive wage-earning labor on the part of the prisoners with study and other forms of culture and character building. All prisoners shall hereafter be treated as human beings who

124

have gone astray and not as criminals undergoing punishment.

• • • • • •

Charles J. Bushnell
"The Place of Religion in Modern Life" (1913)

The actual rapid development of social solidarity—of inter-dependence—through the industrial revolution and its consequences...is rapidly bringing to the foreground of reflective thought the concept of society as organic, in a deeper sense than that of the earlier crude analogies between society and the physical organism of a plant or animal. In the new organic concept (though for that matter older even than the writings of Paul) we are coming to interpret society as composed of inter-dependent members, social by their very nature, specialized in function, and co-operating together for the attainment of the general end of democracy...This conception has developed rapidly within the last dozen or fifteen years.

. . . . . .

The rapid transformation of social customs within the past century, moreover, has enforced the conviction that society is not in any sense fixed but is evolving...From the point of view of the older philosophy and religion of authority, reality and truth are fixed and unchanging, and only man's apprehension of knowledge of them is growing. But the consciousness of men today has violently revolted against this view...Men are convinced that evolution is real—that absolutely new values are being constantly produced in the world by the constructive activity of men—that progress is not an illusion and a sham, but that the blood and struggle of earth's martyrs and toilers have made positive contributions to the universe—that the Christian doctrine of the dignity of personality is a vindicated fact—that aristocracy is blasphemy against Personality—and that democracy, as the ideal of a thoroughly organic society, is the only tenable view of the world order. There is no other way to interpret the growing modern revolt against external, arbitrary authority, and the passion for democracy. Where the religious leaders try to enforce the old view, they are failing; and where they adopt the new view, they are succeeding!

. . . . . .

(W)ith our convictions of the organic nature and evolution of the world, we are being logically forced to the further conviction that any such thing as real growth, even of truth, means a reconstruction of it as an instrument to meet essentially new conditions of life...In other words, the view of truth which is gaining currency today makes it thoroughly a teleological instrument.

. . . . . .

Another striking practical tendency of our time which emphasizes this same change of world view is the rapid spread of philanthropy, and the new sense of sympathy. If we are really organically related, and thus each needful for the welfare of all, then every human being is worthy of respect as a person, as a comrade, however humble, co-operating, or created to co-operate, in the very construction, advancement, and enrichment of the universe. It is this conception which accounts for the growing sense of dignity of the individual, and the angry protest of increasing millions when that dignity is outraged.

126

. . . . . .

[T]he wider contacts of individuals and groups with diverse peoples and customs today are bringing about a cosmopolitanism of tastes and a tolerance of judgments which are further signs of the coming realization of the larger democracy. This enlargement of the perceptions and intellectual apprehensions of mankind is resulting in a remarkable, deepened sense of the psychical, and a remarkable development of the phases of religion heretofore neglected by a traditional Christianity.

• • • • • •

L.C. Gray
"The Economic Possibilities of Conservation" (1913)

Society is confronted by the same choice that accumulation imposes on the individual: a choice between present satisfaction and future satisfaction. Moreover, conservation requires that individuals lessen their consumption today in order that other individuals may enjoy the results of their abstinence. Hence, in so far as it involves the saving for the enjoyment of other generations what we might use for ourselves, it constitutes a type of ethical requirement which is upon a higher level than any that has heretofore existed, — an ethical requirement entirely novel in its scope. The ethical field is to be widened to include unborn generations; not only those which will appear in the immediate future but also those which are yet enshrouded in a future limited only by the uncertain period of human life upon the earth. Few individuals have achieved an ethical level sufficiently exalted to induce them to curtail present enjoyment for the sake of shadowy generations yet to come. Let any policy be imposed at the present day the consequences of which are recognized by the general public as resulting in serious curtailment of present enjoyments in the interest of a most distant future; and one would not have to be a cynic to predict an uprising of the individual against the organs of social control.

The primary problem of conservation, therefore, expressed in economic language, is the determination of the proper rate of discount on the future with respect to the utilization of our natural resources. Some discount of the future, there must be. If society reduced the discount on the future to zero, the period of utilization would be increased to infinity; and therefore, the amount of present use would become infinitesimal. Conservation as a single principle of action involves the equal importance of future wants and present wants. It requires that the want of the infinitely distant future shall be as important as the want of the immediate present. Conservation as a single principle of action is reduced to an absurdity.

Where is the proper balance between utilization and conservation? Philosophically considered, the question cannot be answered with finality without such a definite comprehension of the purpose of human existence as has not been vouchsafed the race. In the absence of more infallible foundations we shall doubtless lean on the "crutch of common sense." Certainly, most of us would agree that utilization must not be so restricted as either to impair the treasured results of past progress or to handicap seriously the rate of progress in the future.

. . . . . .

Altho there is a close connection between the utilization of natural resources and the rapidity of social progress, the connection is by no means so complete as at first appears. Exploitation results in maximum production under certain conditions, but maximum production does not necessarily mean progress. A bad system of distribution may produce a degraded proletariat dominated by an equally degraded plutocracy. Maximum production may be accompanied by a manner of life which is not consistent with the highest social development. A bad distributive system may demand more rapid production, and therefore a more rapid utilization of the resources of society, without bringing to the great majority of our people the satisfactions which rational and legitimate present needs appear to justify. A vast amount of consumption is neither based on welfare, nor on enjoyment; it is solely dictated by convention. The enormous waste of coal required for the electrical advertising in our great cities is illustrative of this exploitative consumption. As Professor H.J. Davenport has expressed it, "Every great White Way in every American city is nightly one more chemical orgy of waste, a crime of competitive advertising for which some day thousands of individuals must shiver for months."

• • • • • •

John C. Kimball,
The Romance of Evolution (1913)

Nature is not doing much in our day at making mountains or continents or seas, or new species of animals or plants or men,—not doing much directly at improving the individual body or bones or even brain. But she is at work now as never before, on the world's social structure, is building up the individual human brick...We think sometimes we would like to look back into the eons of the past and see our material earth, its seas and shores and living things actually evolving under nature's plastic touch; but we can, if we will, do better than that,—see our social earth, its grander shores and finer life, visibly taking shape before our eyes; be, if we will, partners with nature in the work.

. . . . . .

What will be the nature of society's better coming state? Nearly all dreamers have answered, material, moral, civil perfection, a state in which all the forces of nature will be in harmonious action, all the problems of society satisfactorily solved, all the ten thousand forms of the world's evil utterly eliminated, and all the races of men freed from anxiety and care, working only as they wish, and healthy, happy and good...But fascinating as in some respects such a vision is, evolution is very far from pointing to it as one ever likely to be realized. Man's present use of the earth, instead of tending to make it a natural garden, is tending more and more to make it a natural waste,—slashing down its forests, burning up its coal, exhausting its soil, poisoning its airs and letting loose its cyclones and floods. Its big wild beasts may be becoming fewer, but how about its little bacteria? Its new West producing larger crops, but what of its old East? Its machinery doing more and more work, but where is its lessening of our human anxieties and cares? Each new discovery brings with it a new danger,—railroad speed, railroad smash-ups, electric dynamos, electric deaths. Each settlement of an old problem reveals a dozen bigger ones to take its place, shows ahead of us from each mountain climbed...No: evolution does not promise to take us forward to an Eden in the future any more than backwards to one in the past...

But it does promise with its unfolding around us of more difficulties, more evils, more problems to be met, to unfold within us strength and skill for their meeting and more success in winning out of them food, health, happiness, manhood. It is this which has been its trend all through the past,—not fewer foes and battles, but more victories and spoils; not smaller apples and snakes as the tempters, but stronger Adams and Eves as the resisters; not the earth unmade a wilderness, but the earth out of its very wildernesses made to bloom as Eden never did; not its strata of coal undiminished down below, but its layers of the lightning tapped and mined up above; not man less liable to disease, but man endowed by his very wrestlings against disease with a health such as nature never gave; not society without a hell, but society using its hells to make out of them and make for itself, an ever finer heaven. And everything points to this as its direction still more grandly in the future...And while vaster and vaster problems will continually follow his solution of the old ones, the vaster and vaster strength that he will get from their solving, will make him look back on those which to-day are so puzzling,—the silver question, the tariff question, the adjustment of labor and capital, the management of big cities and big hats, and the like,—very much as the man of sixty now does on his childish wrestlings with a, b, ab, and two and two make four. Meliorism, not optimism, an ever bettering, not an ever best, that is the principle, that the promise of evolution, as regards the world's coming social state.

And after all, is not that what we really want, that the thing which really is best? Who dreads difficulty, toil, sacrifice, agony, when to meet them he has health, muscle, courage, brain,—who, rather, does not welcome them as manhood's truest joy? A perfect world to dwell in would mean to its dwellers inevitably the wasting away through ease, of their long, toil-won powers. It is only imperfection which can keep alive perfection...[I]t is an immense satisfaction to feel that evolution will never cease, at least in this world, to provide us amply with manhood's meat of sorrow, hardship, and care,—great problems to be solved for humanity, and great sacrifices to be made for those we love,—never cease, therefore, to give us a betterness in which souls can grow.

. . . . . .

There are three great stages in all evolution, whether it be of worlds, plants, animals, or society, homogeneity, or sameness; that in which everything is in common, as a nebula, a seed, an animalcule; then differentiation or diversifying, that in which the common mass is divided, subdivided and divided again into a multitude of distinct parts, as with planets, the limbs of a tree and the organs of the human body; and finally integration or organization, that in which the parts while still remaining as distinct as ever in their own forms and functions, are joined by their common life principle in a large and complex whole which is capable of functions infinitely beyond what either the original mass or the divided parts could accomplish, as the solar system, the fruit growing tree and the marvelous human body. Now society, like everything else, began in homogeneity, or sameness...and to go back to it would be like the limbed tree's going back to its common trunk, or the starred universe to its undivided fire-mist. Evolution is not traveling at all that way...But while State socialism...is...thus hopeless under evolution, there is another kind of socialism, that of voluntary individual association, the integration of society's differentiated parts not by outward authority, but through their own inherent law, into grand organic wholes, which, as being in the very line of all evolution,—its third great stage following naturally after that of differentiation,—is sure more and more to come about.

. . . . . .

Evolution affords no indication that society's separations...are ever, as some hope, to be closed up, and all men be of the same tastes, caliber, political opinion and religious faith,—tends, rather, to accentuate their existing divisions...But evolution does indicate the coming of a time when out of their separations, here, the same as everywhere else, its other principle of integration shall arise, under which all harsh feeling between them shall pass away, and an organic union take its place, in which their very differences shall be each other's help.

. . . . . .

While nations, also, so far as feature, custom, character and capacity go, will always remain distinct members of the world's great social structure. Nature has not spent such countless ages and such outpourings of blood, treasure and hate in evolving them as separate peoples only to end in resolving them all back again into one conglomerate humanity. But differentiation here, as everywhere else in evolution, will be followed by an integration of the parts that will utilize their very diversities in building out of them a grand organic unity which each people by keeping alive its special entity will render the more complete. Nationality, as we know it now, bristling with bayonets and centered in self, is but a passing phase in humanity's growth; patriotism as it is to-day, fed on battle memories and beautiful with an outward red, white, and blue, but a single petal in the flower of a people's love.

. . . . . .

Human beings were meant to be not mere idle lookers-on in this part of nature's work,—not mere passive blocks waiting to be built by others hands into the coming social state, but live helpers in its doing...And to give this help wisely and well they evidently must know something of what nature's plans are, see something of what nature is aiming to bring about.

. . . . . .

So with evolution set to convoy all the myriad interests of earth from the port of the past to the haven of the world's better coming state. The storms and convulsions of time's sea and the awful night of the grave may indeed fall upon them and drive them wide apart,—make it look sometimes as if all were to be lost. But signaled by their convoy what course to take, and each doing its own best, they, too, shall weather all their storms, survive all their nights, and borne along by nature's mighty flood tide, flood not for six hours merely, but for six million years, reach at last, even the slowest, dullest sailer of them all, the port of the World's Coming Better Social State.

• • • • • •

Graham Wallas
The Great Society (1914)

During the last hundred years the external conditions of civilised life have been transformed by a series of inventions which have abolished the old limits to the creation of mechanical force, the carriage of men and goods, and communication by written and spoken words. One effect of this transformation is a general change of social scale. Men find themselves working and thinking and feeling in relation to an environment, which, both in its world-wide extension and its intimate connection with all sides of human existence, is without precedent in the history of the world.

. . . . . .

Fifty years ago the practical men who were bringing the Great Society into existence thought, when they had time to think at all, that they were...offering an enormously better existence to the whole human race. Men were rational beings, and, having obtained limitless power over nature, would certainly use it for their own good...Now, however, that the change has come, hardly any one thinks of it with the old undoubting enthusiasm. Actual famine has, it is true, disappeared from the Great Society, but there remains the constant possibility of general and uncontrollable depressions of trade. The intervals between great wars are apparently becoming longer, but never has the expenditure on armaments been so great or the fear of war so constant...The deeper anxiety of our time arises from a doubt, more or less clearly realised, whether that [social] development is itself proceeding on right lines.

. . . . . .

We are forced...now to recognise that a society whose intellectual direction consists only of unrelated specialisms must drift, and that we dare not drift any longer. We stand, as the Greek thinkers stood, in a new world. And because that world is new, we feel that neither the sectional observations of the special student, nor the ever-accumulating records of the past, nor the narrow experience of the practical man can suffice us. We must let our minds play freely over all the conditions of life till we can either justify our civilisation or change it.

. . . . . .

Throughout the politics and literature of the twentieth century one traces this fear, conscious or half conscious, lest the civilisation which we have adopted so rapidly and with so little forethought may prove unable to secure either a harmonious life for its members or even its own stability. The old delight in the "manifest finger of destiny" and "the tide of progress," even the newer belief in the effortless "evolution" of social institutions are gone. We are afraid of the blind forces to which we used so willingly to surrender ourselves. We feel that we must reconsider the basis of our organised life because, without reconsideration, we have no chance of controlling it. And so behind the momentary ingenuities and party phrases of our statesmen we can detect the straining effort to comprehend while there is yet time.

● ● ● ● ● ●

Herbert William Conn
Social Heredity and Social Evolution:
The Other Side of Eugenics (1914)

Are there any great lessons which may be learned from social evolution of the past, that can guide us in our endeavor to direct that evolution in the future?...

We may with absolute certainty expect in the future that social evolution will progress in the direction of greater concentration and greater organization. This is the law of the greatest achievement with the least expenditure, and is absolutely irresistible...

With the growing centralization there will be a parallel development of the worth of the individual...The evident drift of social evolution is to give each individual a larger share in the good things of the world, either by legislation or as a result of modified social conditions. But although this will be the general trend of evolution, it will not be uninterrupted.

Social evolution has not come from the constant advance of any one principle, but as the result of a seesaw. Practically every advance in the condition of man has come from struggle. Constant development in any one line has always meant stagnation. It is only as opposing ideas and opposing beliefs and interests are brought into contact with each other that social evolution has advanced. Rivalry and conflicting interests are necessary for an advance. If we hope for the future advance of the race, we must not aim for the cessation of struggle, for this would mean the end of progress. It has been the conflict of centralization and individualism, the opposition of altruism and egoism, that has caused the advance of man to higher and higher grades of civilization...

Through social heredity, a single individual, though leaving no offspring, may turn the direction of evolution, and have more influence upon mankind than another with numerous progeny. Hence, while emphasis should be placed upon reproductive efficiency, even greater emphasis needs to be placed upon making the individual's life count, since the influence of the individual upon evolution through his life may be far greater than his influence through his offspring...

For the vast and complicated structure of civilization which has been built upon [organic] foundation mankind is responsible, and each person who lives his life among men is responsible for a certain share in shaping the evolution of the future.

The hope for the future must lie largely in the development of the ethical nature...Society not only has been, but must remain, ethical in its tendency and aims. New laws, new customs, new conditions, may all be desirable and all have their influence. But unless they involve as a central factor the elevation of the ethical nature of man, they will be futile in the end from lack of vitality...

. . . . . .

Although in the organic evolution of animals *nature* rather than *nurture* has been the predominant force, in human social evolution *nurture* rather than *nature* has stood foremost. It is not what we are born, but what we become after birth that makes us men: it is not the powers of babes, but what civilization makes of those powers that constitutes the essence of mankind. The future is full of hope.

• • • • • •

Walter E. Weyl
The New Democracy (1914)

If we are now to move toward democracy, it is because we are already moving, or preparing to move, in that direction. Our conscious social actions are but a fulfillment, a sanction, an epilogue; the unconscious social strivings precede and prepare.

That this democratic evolution is already preparing is overlooked by him who runs. The development is too multiform and bewildering, and we are too near. If we fix our gaze at one point in progress, we conclude that results are small. If, however, we look over the field and note progress in a succession of social efforts, we are amazed at our advance…

It requires a historical perspective to make any comparison of present and past. "The heirs of all the ages" are spoilt children, valuing only their very newest toys. An infant born a few generations ago might have been elated over the steam engine; a child born to-day will find the telephone, automobile, and X-ray commonplace. He will think no more of aviation as progress than we regard plowing and arithmetic as valuable social acquisitions.

So great is the insistence of the immediate, that we find it well-nigh impossible to picture the state of, let us say, the workingman of a century ago—of the indentured servant, of the slave of the main who sailed before the mast and was beaten, starved, and "hazed," of the workman arrested for debt, of the child without chance of education. A sunlit haze softens the outline of the past, and inclines us to describe present evil conditions in words which in earlier times had a harsher significance. We sometimes apply to modern labor conditions the word "slavery," without realizing how inapposite is a comparison of our present conditions with the auction block, the forcible separate of families, the willful maiming of slaves, the prohibition of education, and other features of the Southern labor system of 1860.

Similarly, because we are so hypnotized by the glitter of our plutocracy, we fail to see the countervailing developments of the last twenty years in political, industrial, and social life.

. . . . . .

We have never had a Utopia, though we have often dreamed that we were on the verge of one...

The mortal defect of Utopias is that they are too static. The kingdom of heaven on earth is always a permanent, unchanging, perfect, and unutterably stupid place, than which our present society, with all its imperfections, is vastly superior. Utopias break down because they represent attainment, fulfillment. But society does not strive towards fulfillment, but only towards striving. It seeks not a goal, but a higher starting point from which to seek a goal.

Opposed to such utopias our present ideal of a socialized democratic civilization is dynamic. It is not an idyllic state in which all men are good and wise and insufferably contented. It is not a state at all, but a mere direction.

Were we to move into a democratic, socialized civilization, where misery had become as unknown as witchcraft to-day; where the people, educated and in process of education, ruled in their own interest both in industry and in politics; where the common wisdom of a nation was united to solve common problems and work out a common destiny, we should still be faced by problems

new and old. We should carry into the new civilization the
tenacious appetites of to-day. We should struggle along
with human frailties, with a residual ignorance,
perverseness, meanness of outlook, exaggerated egotism.
With the raising of the standard of life we should awaken
new appetites and stimulate present ones. Our racial
hatreds, our inveterate race animosities, would give way
but slowly, so that even in a society advanced in
civilization, lynchings and other horrible reversions to
barbarism might occasionally occur. We may not hug the
illusion of an instantaneous change in the old clinging
evils...For this century we need but take this century's
forward step. If we can extirpate misery, that will be
progress enough.

● ● ● ● ● ●

Ernst Richard
God's Path to Peace (1914)

[U]nobserved and unplanned by human agencies, positive
and constructive forces have been at work...institutions
have been established whose originators pursued
altogether different aims than those embodied in universal
peace. For technical inventions, intended for the facilitation
and acceleration of communication and commerce; for
official international treaties, congresses, institutions,
uniform legislation based on international agreements; for
private international congresses, societies, and institutions,
exchange of the fruits of civilization and culture, they all
had, primarily, special aims of their own; but they all are
united in the service of international convergence,
international organization, and international peace. And so

far as they serve this purpose, so far as they have really established considerable beginnings of world organization, just to this extent this historical evolution is not "man's doings," for a conscious, intentional action with international peace in view is not the cause of it...Only in very recent years has the meaning of the forces on which we speak revealed itself to the advocates of peace.

. . . . . .

COINCIDENCES

[S]tarting from different directions, various lines of evolution lead toward the legal and social organization of the world as their common center. It will be seen, furthermore, that all these different currents show a certain synchronism in their different stages of progress—new political or technical achievements signaling, as a rule, an advance along all lines. So follows, for instance, the first modern arbitration treaty in 1794 shortly after the advent of modern democracy with the American and French Revolutions; or after the first steamboat has arrived we soon have the important advance in international legislation as to slave trade and the neutrality of Switzerland by the Vienna Congress. The first steam railroad and the first crossing of the ocean by a steamship is contemporaneous with the important Congresses of London about 1830 and the first Copyright Treaty. The very same year that sees the first opening of an international railroad witnesses also the first (private) world's congress (1843). The first cable crosses the ocean about the time when that other epochal international congress and the first World's Fair are held in Paris. The final national consolidation of the United States, Germany, and Italy precedes immediately the organization of the Universal Postal Union; the invention of wireless telegraphy and the opening of the Institute of Agriculture in Rome occur about the same time. These are only a few of the most striking parallelisms of facts independent of each other, and still indicating the workings of a universal law. In our days events of this character are so frequent that they might be shown from month to month and their parallelism has lost its striking character.

. . . . . .

Does not the work and the aim of the advocates of peace, so often the object of ridicule, take an entirely new aspect when we see that instead of chasing after Utopian dreams of the future, they rather have failed to see that they were overtaken by the actual stage of evolution of civilized society? That they have tried to achieve along one single line what in many fields has become a fact already?

. . . . . .

Get Together! This is the command urged upon all mankind to-day; this is the goal toward which the eternal forces of human progress irresistibly converge. In them we must confide, in them the guarantee is given of rescue from the inferno through which we are passing to-day. They will guide us safely to happiness and justice.

● ● ● ● ● ●

Jessie Taft
The Woman Movement from the Point of View of Social Consciousness (1915)

The degree of social consciousness which humanity shall be able to attain depends directly on the number of individuals who succeed in becoming conscious of the full meaning of all their social relations, who recognize to the full their dependence on a social situation for the form of self they develop, and who increasingly multiply the number of social attitudes or selves which they are capable of maintaining towards these complex relationships. When a majority of the members of a society become thus socially conscious, we shall have conditions favorable for the control of social problems since all the elements involved will be explicitly present in the consciousness of the majority of individuals. But this stage of social development can never be reached as long as any large class of people, such as its women, are permitted, encouraged, or forced to exist in an unreal world willfully maintained for that purpose. Nor will the selves of men, in so far as they are formed by their relations to women, ever reach the full possibilities of selfhood while women remain only partially self-conscious.

• • • • • •

Patrick Geddes
Cities in Evolution (1915)

Despite our contemporary difficulties—industrial, social, and political,—there are available around us the elements of a civic uplift, and with this, of general advance to a higher plane of industrial civilisation. The civic awakening and the constructive effort are fully beginning, in healthy upgrowth, capable not only of survival but of fuller cultivation also, towards varied flower and fruit-flower in regional and civic literature and history, art, and science; fruit in social renewal of towns and cities, small and great.

Such renewal involves ever-increasing domestic and individual well-being, and these a productive efficiency, in which art may again vitalise and orchestrate the industries, as of old.

. . . . . .

With civic energies and life thus renewing from within, and the bettered condition of the people kept clearly in view, the interior circulation and the larger communications from without will become all the clearer, and be surer than before of constructive efficiency and artistic effect. For civic considerations have to illuminate and control geographic ones, as well as conversely. Idealism and matter of fact are thus not sundered, but inseparable, as our daily steps are guided by ideals of direction, themselves unreachably beyond the stars, yet indispensable to getting anywhere, save indeed downwards. Eutopia, then, lies in the city around us; and it must be planned and realised, here or nowhere, by us as its citizens—each a citizen of both the actual and the ideal city seen increasingly as one.

● ● ● ● ● ●

James Henry Ecob
"Studies in Social Christianity: Interdependence" (1915)

The world is just beginning to understand that the interdependencies of its intellectual life are just as deeply founded and imperative as the multiple, involved conditions of its material life. One can no more think through a day than he can furnish his table without laying the ends of the earth under tribute. A woman in France discovers radium. Instantly the whole civilized world is ablaze with excitement. Scientists in all lands are readjusting their thinking. Our conceptions of matter are revolutionized—all things are radio-active. A man in India discovers that plants are sensitive through and through and doubtless have a degree of consciousness. Instantly we are all beginning to look out upon the miracle of life with eyes touched to a new and compelling vision never before imagined, except as a poet's dream.

• • • • • •

Florence Guertin Tuttle
The Awakening of Woman (1915)

[The woman's movement] is an inner revolution before it is an outer revolt, subjective before objective. All the recent unprecedented activities of women have been but manifestations of this inner quickening. Arising from interior necessity, they are but symbols of a spiritual revolution sweeping the sisterhood of the earth. They are the result of cause and effect, of action and reaction on a psychic plane. Any view less comprehensive than this spiritually inclusive view is superficial, and therefore imperfect.

What occasioned the feminist movement? Throughout the ages the life of woman, from evolutionary necessity, was one of hard labor, almost exclusively physical. Before woman could develop psychically it was necessary that she should first be freed from the obligation of the world's drudgery. The invention of machinery was the real emancipator of woman's spiritual energies, bestowing an unprecedented leisure. The privileges of the higher education, granted in the middle of the last century, awoke the feminine brain cell and released woman's intellectual faculties. For the primitive occupations of woman, it must be remembered, while absorbing her complete attention, did not directly exercise or develop her mind. There was no specific training of the feminine intellect. The projecting cause of the woman's movement, then, was a stimulated mentality.

. . . . . .

What is not generally comprehended in the present is, as has been noted, that the universal awakening of woman to-day, with its consequent stirring of mentally creative powers, is also nature's call for race advancement. The time has arrived when mankind requires a freer, more developed womanhood; when, through the agency of mechanical invention and the smaller family that is considered of modem social advantage, all the energies of woman are no longer required upon a material plane; when spiritually creative qualities are racially the most desirable to be developed and transmitted, and must be so transmitted if we are to have a progressively evolving posterity. For it is as logical as the conclusion of a mathematical theorem: a developed imagination in the mothers must be followed by a developed imagination in the race.

. . . . . .

It is not a coincidence that civilization has advanced more in the last hundred years than in the previous thousand— ever since, in fact, it decided to give intellectual and spiritual opportunities to its women.

. . . . . .

The ideals of each age change. And the parents of every age must improve if racial stagnation, or, worse still, degeneration, is not to ensue. Our mothers were good enough for us, we say, and so they were. But they are not good enough for our children any more than we should be adequate parents for the children of 1930. The qualifications of motherhood are not static. In fact, no other relationship calls for such plasticity, such fluidity to reflect the spirit of the times, and to move with it, as motherhood.

. . . . . .

Because the warrior ideal is passing, the charge has been made that the world has become feminized, and that the prevalence of women school-teachers is causing the manly virtues to become extinct. If this is true, may it not be that civilization is endeavoring to teach us to alter our definition of manly? Most of the outrages in history were "manly." May we not possibly pursue some of the "feminine" virtues without losing virility? The modern dentist advises: "Be brave—be a woman." It requires more courage, more fortitude, to face motherhood once than a cannon a dozen times. To be feminine is not always to be soft—though man is pleased to cherish the illusion. To be feminine may be to be lion-hearted—and then not to talk about it!

. . . . . .

Unrest is not a crime. Unrest is a symptom of growth. Just how much the unrest of women has had to do with evolving the new ideals that are characterizing the age will never be known. Nor is it important that it should be known. The significant thing for men and women to recognize is that a new valuation has been placed on life and must be maintained by them working together. Feminism is not anti-man. Feminism is pro-man. The conservation of life is human, racial business, not of one sex, but of both.

It is not surprising that little value was attached to human life in the past since human waste is one of the most ancient ideas and biological in foundation. For countless ages human evolution progressed, like lower animal evolution, through the sacrifice of untold millions.

...To-day we are witnessing the beginning of an almost universal revolt against wasteful human expenditure. Is it an accident that this protest, this revaluation of life, has followed so quickly the social awakening of women? Does the character of the woman's movement contain elements that equip her for this unprecedented crusade?

. . . . . .

Every new idea is called Utopian until proved of greater practical value than the old. The plan of free schools, free playgrounds, free hospitals, free social service was once all considered Utopian. Humanity progresses only as the whole army of mankind is enabled to move forward, usually by so-called Utopian tactics. The Utopian is the spiritual, and the spiritual is the practical for a species evolving on a psychical plane.

● ● ● ● ● ●

William Pickens
The New Negro (1916)

The progress of a race cannot be measured day after day, but must be taken decade after decade, or generation after generation. Has the Negro advanced? Fifty years ago he did not own his own body; now he owns a billion dollars besides. Then he was a man without a country, hardly claiming a foot of land; now he has three hundred thousand farms, half a million homes and half a hundred banks. Then he was ignorant; now he has thirty thousand schools with more than thirty thousand teachers, and half a dozen millions who can read. He always had religion, but now, in addition to that, he has about thirty thousand churches with millions of members and the Lord only knows how many preachers.

...The black American should advance faster in the future than in the past, for nothing succeeds like success. But if it should take two years of the future to equal one year of the past, it would not justify despair. In 1837 Lovejoy was murdered in Illinois for a mild opinion against Negro slavery; in 1863 a man of Illinois issued a proclamation freeing millions of Negroes. In 1857 the highest court in the land expressed an opinion that the Negro had no more respectable rights than the beasts of the field; and a little more than ten years later the Negro was made a citizen by the highest law in the land. Fifty years ago if a book was found in the hands of a Negro, that hand might be cut off with a carpenter's tool; while to-day he has thousands of schools and millions of students. There is absolutely no reason in despair.

. . . . . .

[W]e are all, white and black, subjects of circumstances, children of antecedents over which we have no control. The present is the offspring of the past. We have been cast up as a mountain is cast up from the deep, and it will take time to alter our relation to one another and to the rest of the world. Tho all is not well, and tho the changes of a day are invisible, yet the decades and the ages are telling and will tell the story of our progress and mutual adjustment. Race prejudice is simply the last great enemy of human brotherhood, and in its turn it will be destroyed as have all the other enemies. It is simply the last barrier behind which the retreating narrowness of the human heart has taken refuge. All other bars to universal brotherhood have been broken one by one: First, man tried to live to himself; every man's hand was against his neighbor, and he scarcely trusted even the female with whom he associated. This isolating prejudice was finally broken down and he acquired an interest in certain other individuals, his family. But it was family against family now. Intermarriage brought families into alliances, and retreating prejudice took its next stand behind the clan-family,—and it was clan against clan, and finally tribe against tribe. It is now nation against nation and league against league. Will it later be race against race and color against color? The lines of civilization are surely drawing closer against the grim and ancient caste of race prejudice. And whether it comes as a sequal to gigantic interracial conflict or through the long siege of intellectual, moral and religious forces, it seems certain that the overthrow of this last enemy will mark the establishment of Universal Human Brotherhood.

. . . . . .

It is hard for some white men to think of the black man other than as either a useful thing or a nuisance. They cannot conceive him as a thinking, self-active agent pursuing his own ends. As a free man he must put thought in front of his work and industry. He must think first and act afterwards. As a member of the body politic, instead of a mere tool thereof, he must cultivate the intellect, which is the guide both to the hand and to the heart. The intellect is the dynamo, the hand is the motor; it is also one of the eyes of conscience. The mind of man is his pathfinder in industry and in moral prudence: it is the most lordly and admirable thing in the human world. Nothing is great in the world but man, nothing great in man but mind. It has searched the inscrutable past and prophesied the unsearchable future. It has delved to the center of the earth and mounted to the invisible star. It has taken the rocks of the earth as the pages of a ponderous book and has read therein the history of the prehistoric age and the records of a manless world. From the scattered bones of the solitary plains it has reconstructed, clothed in flesh and revived the ancestor of man and beast. With its daring hand it has caught the loud-threatening thunderbolt, tamed it and made of it a willing messenger. In its magic hand it catches the ray of light that has fled from the verge of the universe and compels it to "reveal the secrets" of its far-off home. Standing in the present it links the past and future, projects and extends the life of an individual man over milleniums of history, and it re-thinks the very thoughts of God.

• • • • • •

Gustav Spiller
"The Interpretation of Sociological Data" (1916)

With man...a novel and momentous factor enters in biological evolution—dependence on the material and other inventions and discoveries of virtually all the members of his race from the earliest times to his own. From this ensues...that he depends on completest culture for completest living and that he will therefore be able to realize himself fully only when the quality and the quantity of this fund of thought have reached infinity.

. . . . . .

[R]easoning from the past to the future, we appear justified in concluding that with the ages collective or pan-human thought leads necessarily—

a) to an almost infinite growth of material and other inventions and discoveries;
b) to an almost infinite improvement of these;
c) to a complete equalization of economic, political, moral, intellectual, aesthetic, and other advantages among individuals and peoples; and
d) to humanity becoming a single organized co-operative totality...

The suggested definition of man also implies—

a) the existence of societies or communities, the individual being wholly unfitted by nature to live by himself;
b) the innate mental and moral equality of individuals, sexes, families, classes, castes, nations, and races, from which follows the demand for equal opportunities and treatment;
c) the need to provide thorough home and school education for all—physical, intellectual, moral, aesthetic, civic, and vocational;
d) science becoming man's guiding genius in all spheres of life and on an equal basis;
e) the indispensability of co-operation in all spheres of life and on an equal basis;
f) the need for institutions which shall store the accumulations of the past, present, and future—e.g., government, law, marriage, etc.

g) equal respect for past, present, and future, or for conservatism, presentism, and futurism (which might be merged into pan-temporism);

h) as the supreme end the striving collectively and individually to promote the cause of the ideal, and a sense of oneness with all humanity, of which the individual is but an expression;

i) as a rule of conduct and action the exhibiting in all the relationships of life of a profound fellow-feeling, guided by fullest information and circumspect thought, accompanied by geniality and refinement, and intelligently realized by strenuous and firm-bent will— the mind acting as a whole;

j) and respect for the fundamental needs—hunger, exercise, etc.

• • • • • •

William John Meredith
The Evolution of Democracy (1916)

[D]emocratic cooperation is really the law of all evolution. The survival of the fittest does not mean the triumph of the fighter or the plunderer, but of the fittest cooperator with his kind and with the other kindly things of the universe. When the last king and priest and lawyer are a curious historical memory, man will still be patiently climbing toward a more perfect co-partnership...

. . . . . .

To one who has studied the evolution of democracy, it is not hard to predict the future line of development. It must be toward more active, more intimate and more intelligent

154

and personally responsible participation by every citizen in political matters,—not in office holding particularly, for more and more the official servant of the people will come to be an expert non-partizan manager or clerk,—but in actual legislation, in steady, consistent law-enforcing by intelligently moral public program, less and less in "thou shalt nots" and penalty.

. . . . . .

What are the greater problems of the immediate future? Among many these five seem to be most insistently clamoring for solution:

I. The establishment of social justice by intelligent control of unemployment, elimination of profit in vice, minimizing of crime by humane treatment of social victims, education out of the mental habit of lawlessness by simplifying laws, suppression of attorneys and rationalizing court procedure.

II. Recognition of woman's true social function and economic status. That is to say, we must treat them as human adults with equal responsibility, equal rights, equal duties, regardless of sex, all questions of employment to be decided as now among men according to the mental and physical fitness of the individual, doing away with the hypocrisy and insult of "chivalry," and all that foolish patter of the natural subordination of the female.

III. The protection, care and culture of the child, every child, as the state's paramount duty, throughout all accidental gradations of society, with full consciousness that the foundling of to-day may be the people's highest servant of the morrow, that as each generation guards its young, so will the next fulfill the hope of the race.

IV. The abolition of poverty and the slum by that intelligent cooperation which shall insure to every human being food and warmth at least as the simplest, cheapest and safest provision we can make for the physical happiness of all, for the development of individual genius, for the elevation of common morality and emancipation of man from the base fear which lies at the root of all injustice.

V. The eradication of disease through scientific investigation at public expense, isolation of communicable plagues, sterilization of degenerates, national education in healthful living and hygienic responsibility.

It is a big program when viewed pessimistically or selfishly, but there is nothing in it physically impossible, and surely no expense or labor would be too great, now that we see the need. Less than this no man who loves his kind or values the happiness of his own descendants can, without shame, approve. That it must come in time no one who has studied the evolution of democracy can doubt. Why not begin now to win this great and crowning triumph of man's long climb upward, so as to clear the way for a more glorious vision than any man has yet beheld?

• • • • • •

Evander Bradley McGilvary
"The Warfare of Moral Ideals" (1916)

An ideal is not a cold idea; it is heated in the flame of passion, else it were no ideal. It is what we yearn for, not what we passively contemplate. A moral ideal is a glowing vision of conduct and of social life, such as we burn to see realised. It is our ardour for it that converts it from what it would otherwise be, an idle reverie, into a dynamic force...As to the uncertainty of the realisation of our ideals...It is cowardly not to make an effort to get what we want, if the failure is due merely to the fact that we are not sure of success. When human nature shall have lost its venturesomeness, when only certainties attract and all uncertainties leave us unnerved, then indeed it will be time to fear a view that makes the realization of our moral ideals problematic. Meanwhile, there is zest in the very fact that something precious is at stake and may be lost or won...All we need is *not* to know that the end is unattainable, and to believe that there is a chance for success.

. . . . . .

We are concerned with the question what we should like to be, what we should like to help our children to become, what kind of civilisation we shall lend our efforts to build up for the future. The fundamental question to be answered before any question about progress can be answered is the most momentous question in the world for us as moral agents. The question is *what we really want*. This is not a question to be answered lightly. Knowledge of all sorts is of help in answering it, especially knowledge of the consequences of getting what we want. But when all the knowledge is got that can be got, when we have obtained as clear vision as with our human limitations we can obtain, still we shall find ourselves passively contemplating a wan and colourless future unless our desires rise up to seize some envisaged possibility and invest it with the charm of the ideal. That which we prefer above all else when we know all that we can know about it, that for us is best. Movement in the direction of this our enlightened preference is progress; movement away from it is retrogression. To a man with active preferences, progress is not an illusion, because his preferences are indubitable fact. The only illusion is in supposing that a preference of his own is the universe's choice, that a fact here and now is a revelation of what the universe is at bottom and at all times.

• • • • • •

Morton Prince
"A World Consciousness and Future Peace" (1916)

What hope does psychology hold out to civilization? The common ideals of a collective consciousness respect and protect the rights of individuals and regulate their relations to one another within the nation. May it not be that, with time, fostered by systematic worldwide teaching, there may be developed an international consciousness, or world consciousness so far as concerns international relations? And may it not be that the principles of such a consciousness will regulate the nations in their relations to one another to the same extent that the social and national consciousness within a single nation regulate the relations of the people to one another, and, in the United States today, the relations of the sovereign states of the American Union to one another? In such a world consciousness there would grow up common habits of mind that would become second nature—common points of view, common ideals of right and wrong in the dealings of one nation with another.

Likewise conceptions of humanity, of liberty and of the obligations of one people to another would have a common meaning, which is not the case today...The imponderable force of such a consciousness would offer the strongest support to international law—the power behind the law,—

and out of such ideals and such desires, when established, there would necessarily develop a general will to peace and a will to fulfil the obligations imposed by the ideals.

Theoretically the attainment of a world consciousness of this kind is psychologically possible…To reach such an end the old-world habit of mind—the habit of thinking in war-terms, of turning at first thought to war as a necessary means of settling international disputes, must be broken…If such a world consciousness should be developed, one nation will understand another because the ideals of the common consciousness will have the same meaning.

…A world consciousness in international relations— that is the vision I see, the dream that psychology permits us to have. May the dream come true!

• • • • • •

C.L. Vestal
"The Meaning of American Democracy" (1917)

Only a machine civilization can be standardized in detail, and one of the aims of democracy is to emancipate us from our present thraldom to machine civilization.

. . . . . .

Democracy seeks to instil a faith that intelligence, informed by patriotic feeling, can solve the great problems of the world. Though democracy is evolution, it is conscious evolution.

• • • • • •

George V. Kracht
"Social Ideals and Social Progress" (1917)

In the individual, growth from unconsciousness to consciousness marks the line of evolution. Social evolution, likewise, is progression from instinctive to intelligent action...The appearance of a new social ideal is a psychical variation, as truly a product of the evolutionary process as any physical modification of structure. The formula of evolution must be broad enough to include ethical man.

. . . . . .

As intelligence and will emerge from their obscurity, and the individuals of the race become more or less self-determining, the social organism, likewise, rises above an existence, whose activities are determined by unconscious forces, and becomes to some extent a self-determining entity; a being which realizes its ends through carefully selected means...Many ages must elapse before the most important factor in social evolution is conscious action towards definite ideals. For the present, we must rest content with the fact that steady progress is being made towards such a state...

• • • • • •

Patrick Geddes
Ideas at War (1917)

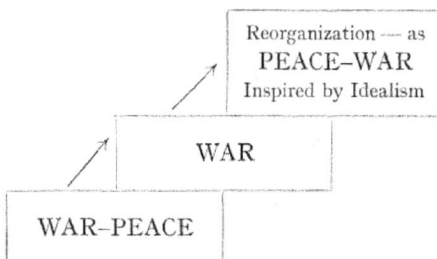

Reorganization — as
PEACE–WAR
Inspired by Idealism

WAR

WAR–PEACE

The nature of the problem of Reconstruction in the world is indicated immediately by the criticism of the world as it is. It is to secure the passage out of the Mechanical-Imperial-Financial Age into an age which without letting slip what has been gained of real, human, value by mechanical invention, imperial organization, and the international network of financial relations, shall yet win for it those essentials of a saner, nobler and happier human life which have most conspicuously been deficient...

. . . . . .

The great deficiency of the Mechanical Age is its sacrifice of Life to Things. Therefore the first effort for the new age must be to make it eutechnic: not only must physical health bulk more largely in our minds than the possession of commodities endowed with exchange values, but also physical health and well-being must be regarded as important and valuable mainly as a condition of the inner life of the soul.

. . . . . .

The present age being Imperialistic, the new age must aim at being Geotechnic: that is, we must regard the world not as something to be administered and exploited, but as something to be cared for, as the gardener converts a waste patch into an oasis of beauty and fertility.

. . . . . .

Lastly, the effort of the new age must be Neotechnic, instead of Financial. Anthropologists divide the Stone Age into the Palaeolithic period of rude flint axes and a savage, possibly cannibalistic, hunting life, and the Neolithic Age of daintily polished flint arrow-heads, which saw also the taming of all our common domestic animals and the beginning of the culture of the soil. Similarly, we may divide the age of Machinery into the palaeotechnic age of smoke and the steam engine, and the neotechnic age of electricity and radium, of finer implements, the conquest of noise, and the utilization of waste. Nor need this be slow, because every mechanic and engineer in the country is conscious of the fact that we need to pass from the present to the neotechnic stage, and his ambition is to do something to help through the transition.

. . . . . .

In the clear sunlight, then, of ethics, politics and science regenerated and socialized from those of the mechanical-imperial phase, we may go forward anew, as of old — to reshape each city and region, so that men may again lead and share "the good life," and express all in them that is most human.

• • • • • •

A. Lincoln Greenlaw
Resident Forces of Life, The Evolution of Humanity (1917)

***The ideal of intelligent thought is not post-mortem self-consciousness and ineffable felicity; unconnected with and contradictory to every condition of life's appearance and continuance.

***It is rather that of personal character and activity; social democratic government; ethical and practical education of childhood and youth; and world-wide international peace and comity.

***This age must evolve a new, a Racial Conscience. It necessitates Racial Men; world statesmanship; ethical Leaders, in every department and enterprise of humanity.

***The tariff of superstition's monopoly must be lifted from the understanding and conscience of men, opening to earth's multitudes the new world of personal intelligence, moral responsibility, and mental freedom, all founded upon human nature and mutual relationships.

***Rapid transit; instantaneous communication of thought and intelligence; world-wide commerce, and the great industries upon which it depends; combined, on the other hand, with modern engines of destruction and desolation, compel a type of world-manhood, and citizenship impossible to any preceding generation.

***Scientific achievement has not only opened the way thereto; but necessitates that men—and nations—shall walk therein; at the peril of civilization's decline and decay.

***It is primarily a matter of your personal decision and action.

***As wise Men, Judge Ye.

. . . . . .

VI

Organization culminates
With form, endowed to sustain
Nature's energy and record;
In her storage batt'ry-brain.

Man is nature's evolution
Into personality;
Recognizing self-awareness,
Conscious of immensity:—

Microcosm of nature's vastness;
Record of her ceaseless play;
Student of her hither progress;—

Prophet of all future sway.

Universal cosmic forces;
Solar systems in their way;
Planets in their orb'ts revolving,—
Have their type in human clay.

. . . . . .

CXXXVII

What of the mighty, surging Now?—
Product of all past ages;—
What of psychic force evolving—
Living—in Human Pages?

Synthetic Genesis' cycle,
Has evolved Intellection,
To direct dynamic desires:—
What shall be its direction?

It has harnessed nature's forces,—
Evidencing wise design;
Making the world a neighborhood;
Mankind—Neighbors;—Yours and Mine.

It has developed industry;
Art, science, trade, invention
World-wide;—of human endeavor.
What—of the Church's contention?

Nothing can bridge the wid'ning gulf;
Intellect's—thought's—contention;—
But honest churchmen's concession;—
Church, too,—is Man's convention.

It is time to scrap the outgrown

Of traditionary thought; —
Psychical adolescence's age; —
NOW, — Let living truth be taught.

Let pulpit become a forum;
Dealing with understanding;
MAN — must enthrone Justice and Truth; —
Ethical Force commanding.

Mind cannot conceive future life,
But that of generation.
Concept cannot transcend percept;
NOW, IS MAN'S DAY, — of salvation.

. . . . . .

CXXXIX

Future of race ever depends
Upon the Leaders of Men;
Intelligence determines right;
Fear will never rule again.

Inventions now necessitate
Intelligence's diffusion
To earth's remotest boundaries;
Retiring past illusion.

Man has liberated forces
Destructive of endeavor.
Ethical thought, Race must enthrone,
Or Freedom fails forever.

• • • • •

Mary Parker Follett
The New State (1918)

Conscious evolution means giving less and less place to herd instinct and more to the group imperative. We are emerging from our gregarious condition and are now to enter on the rational way of living by scanning our relations to one another, instead of bluntly feeling them, and so adjusting them that unimpeded progress on this higher plane is secured...We know now that there are no immutable goals—there is only a way, a process, by which we shall, like gods, create our own ends at any moment—crystallize just enough to be of use and then flow on again. The flow of life and we the flow: this is the truth. Life is not a matter of desirable objects here and there; the stream flows on and he who waits with his object is left with a corpse. Man is equal to life at every moment, but he must live for life and not for the things life has produced.

Yet while it is true that life can never be formalized or formulated, that life is movement, change, onwardness, this does not mean that we must give up the abiding. The unchangeable and the unchanging are both included in the idea of growth. Stability is neither rigidity nor sterility: it is the perpetual power of bringing forth.

Writers are always fixing dates for the dividing line between the ancient and the modern world, or between the mediaeval and the modern world. Soon the beginning of modern times, of modern thought, will, I believe, be dated at the moment when men began to look at a plastic world, at a life constantly changing, at institutions as only temporary crystallizations of life forces, of right as evolving, of men as becoming.

The real work of every man is then to build. The challenge is upon us. This is the task to which all valiant souls must set themselves. We are to rise from one mastery to another. We are to be no longer satisfied with the pace of a merely fortuitous progress. We must know now that we are coworkers with every process of creation, that our function is as important as the power which keeps the stars in their orbits. We are creators here and now. We are not in the anteroom of our real life. This is real life.

We cannot, however, mould our lives each by himself; but within every individual is the power of joining himself fundamentally and vitally to other lives, and out of this vital union comes the creative power. Revelation, if we want it to be continuous, must be through the community bond. No individual can change the disorder and iniquity of this world. No chaotic mass of men and women can do it. Conscious group creation is to be the social and political force of the future. Our aim must be to live consciously in more and more group relations and to make each group a means of creating. It is the group which will teach us that we are not puppets of fate.

· · · · · ·

Already the change has begun. I have said that we are beginning to recognize this power—there are many indications that we are beginning to live this power. We are no longer willing to leave human affairs to "natural" control: we do not want war because it is "natural" to fight; we do not want a haphazard population at the dictates of "nature." We no longer believe that sickness and poverty are sent by God; people are being taught that they need not be sick, that it is largely in their own hands, their own collective hands (social hygiene etc.). Modern charity is not aimed at relieving individual poverty, but at freeing the individual from the particular enslavement which has produced his poverty, in freeing society from the causes which produce poverty at all.

Our once-honored blind forces are more and more losing their mastery over us. We are at this moment, however, in a difficult transition period. We are "freer" than ever before; the trouble is we do not know what to do with this freedom. It is easy to live the moral, the "social," life when it consists in following a path carefully marked out for us, but the task given us to-day is to revalue all the world values, to steer straight on and on into the unknown—a gallant forth-faring indeed. But conscious evolution, the endless process of a perfect coordinating, demands vital people. War is the easy way: we take to war because we have not enough vitality for the far more difficult job of agreeing. So also that kind of religion which consists of contemplation of other-worldliness is the easy way, and we take to that when we have not enough vitality deliberately to direct our life and construct our world. It takes more spiritual energy to express the group spirit than the particularist spirit. This is its glory as well as its difficulty. We have to be higher order of beings to do it— we become higher order of beings by doing it. And so the progress goes on forever: it means life forever in the making, and the creative responsibility of every man.

Conscious evolution is the key to that larger view of democracy which we are embracing to-day. The key? Every man sharing in the creative process is democracy; this is our politics and our religion. People are always inquiring into their relation to God. God is the moving force of the world, the ever-continuing creating where men are the co-creators.

"Chaque homme fait dieu, un peu, avec sa vie," as one of the most illumined of the younger French poets says. Man and God are correlates of that mighty movement which is Humanity self-creating. God is the perpetual Call to our self-fulfilling. We, by sharing in the life-process which binds all to-gether in an active, working unity are all the time sharing in the making of the Universe. This thought calls forth everything heroic that is in us; every power of which we are capable must be gathered to this glorious destiny. This is the True Democracy.

• • • • • •

Franklin Bobbitt
The Curriculum (1918)

Since the opening of the twentieth century, the evolution of our social order has been proceeding with great and ever-accelerating rapidity. Simple conditions have been growing complex. Small institutions have been growing large. Increased specialization has been multiplying human interdependencies and the consequent need of coordinating effort. Democracy is increasing within the Nation; and growing throughout the world. All classes are aspiring to a full human opportunity. Never before have civilization and humanization advanced so swiftly.

As the world presses eagerly forward toward the accomplishment of new things, education also must advance no less swiftly. It must provide the intelligence and the aspirations necessary for the advance; and for stability and consistency in holding the gains. Education must take a pace set, not by itself, but by social progress.

The present program of public education was mainly formulated during the conditions of the nineteenth century. In details it has been improved. In fundamentals it is not greatly different. A program never designed for the present day has been inherited.

Any inherited system, good for its time, when held to after its day, hampers social progress. It is not enough that the system, fundamentally unchanged in plan and purpose, be improved in details...Our schools to-day are better than ever before...Improvements are visible on every hand. And yet to do the nineteenth-century task better than it was then done is not necessarily to do the twentieth-century task.

New duties lie before us...Education is now to develop a type of wisdom that can grow only out of participation in the living experiences of men, and never out of mere memorization of verbal statements of facts...We have been developing knowledge, not function; the power to reproduce facts, rather than the powers to think and feel and will and act in vital relation to the world's life. Now we must look to these latter things as well.

• • • • • •

Benchara Branford
A New Chapter in the Science of Government (1919)

A grand process, evolving in each of two opposite directions, yet reinforcing each the other, has been developing gradually throughout the evolutionary ages. Let us call it briefly the *bi-directional* process of spiral evolution. It has an internal form which is *psychic* (mental); and an external form which is *somatic* (corporate). Internally it affects the human soul in all its varieties and forms, the individual soul and the group soul—the soul of the city, the soul of the region, the soul of the nation, the soul of the continent, and the world-soul.

In essence this process consists, in the one direction, of a widening of idea from any given stage outwards till it embraces all the successive *larger* concrete units up to the wide world itself; in the other direction it consists of an enrichment of the idea by an incorporation of all the successive *smaller* concrete units till it embraces the individual. From an internal and psychic standpoint, it embraces the whole social *inheritance;* from an outward and corporate aspect it embraces the whole social *heritage.*

We may regard this process from either a spiritual or a social aspect.

...This grand process of evolution, psychic and corporate, natural and spiritual, has so far, save to a few exceptional individuals, been almost wholly *sub-conscious;* the coming New Era possesses, among other characteristic marks, this additional and profoundly important one that mankind has at length reached a stage when it is rapidly growing increasingly *conscious* of this world-process.

As this consciousness grows more full, wide and vivid, it comes increasingly within the power of mankind to expedite its working, to enrich its contents, to realise its significance, to apply the law to its own further welfare.

Alike politically and spiritually mankind is painfully realising that we are all members of one family.

• • • • • •

G.E. Partridge
The Psychology of Nations (1919)

A study of war ought to help us decide whether we must accept our future, with its possibility of wars, as a kind of fate, or whether we must now begin, with a new idea of conscious evolution, to apply our science and our philosophy and our practical wisdom seriously for the first time to the work of creating history, and no longer be content merely to live it.

• • • • • •

George de Bothezat
"The Meaning for Humanity of the
Aerial Crossing of the Ocean" (1919)

The fate of humanity is in progress; this is why the victory of the "New Humanism" can not be stopped. But let us reach it by the peaceful way of conscious evolution, and not by the way of bloody revolution, whose specter stands ready to spread itself over the earth's surface...[T]he evolution of humanity, although bound up with technical conquests, depends, for the rapidity of its progress, also in a large measure upon social morality. The one brings the other with it.

• • • • • •

Edwin Grant Conklin
"Has Progressive Evolution Come to an End?" (1919)

Finally, a new path of evolution has been found in man by rational cooperation, that is in the further development of human society on a basis of intelligence rather than of instinct. Certainly in this direction the limits of human evolution have not been reached: indeed, it may be said that the rational evolution of society has barely begun. It is a notable fact that the social evolution of man is going forward at a very much more rapid rate than his physical or intellectual evolution…[I]n social organization the most enormous advances have been made, and changes are still going on, at a rate which is amazing if not alarming.

. . . . . .

The future may produce no super-men, but it is likely to produce a super-state and a super-civilization.

. . . . . .

The past evolution of man has occurred almost entirely without conscious human guidance; but with the appearance of intellect and the capacity of profiting by experience, a new and great opportunity and responsibility have been given man of directing rationally and ethically his own evolution.

• • • • • •

Carrie Chapman Catt
"A Christmas Greeting to the New Woman Voter" (1919)

It is not only industrial and social unrest which is the matter with the nation today. It is political failure. For a century our political parties have plowed around serious problems. The neglected problem of slavery brought the Civil War, the neglected problem of buying and selling votes has resulted in secret despotic influences, seeking to control the government. An infinitely bigger question than Are you a

Republican, or Are you a Democrat is, Are you an American? We must stand together to see that our political parties conquer their cowardice and plow through and not around the problems of our national life.

Evolution is certain. What the world needs is evoluters. Evolution moves faster and by more direct methods when it has the aid of evoluters.

We are entering a struggle in which constitutional and political methods of evolution are in conflict with direct methods of revolution. Those who believe in evolution rather than revolution should be up and doing.

• • • • • •

Morrison I. Swift
Can Mankind Survive (1919)

If for a time we could induce all people to study the new social forces at work without heat or prejudice, with unflinching candor, as the surgeon takes an X-ray photograph of a broken bone in order to treat and heal it, the basis of an enlightenment which would save from destruction would be gained. No other method can give us that basis. The old habit of anger at all honest social diagnosis is suicidal. Never before was the world in so evil and wholly perilous a state as now, and the stony pride in iniquity that has controlled the past will prevent a redeeming reorganization of man if it is not broken. Let us therefore proceed as if this pride did not exist and as if modern men were united in the will to produce a world decent and fit to dwell in.

. . . . . .

[I]t is the principal business of society and education and civilized institutions to store all minds with pernicious fat of many varieties and to impress their victims with the sacredness of the deposit. This statement is not in the least figurative. It is an exact description of what human beings have been doing to themselves and their young as far back as we have records. They have been loading themselves with substance of which a large part was rubbish and teaching their children to fill their children with the same. To omit some of this rubbish or to excavate it was the great wickedness.

Thus was formed the habit of unchangingness and nonadaptability. Owing to this fatal habit mankind has remained almost stationary for many thousand years. The *habit of evolution*, that supremely interesting fact connected with life, has never been learned by the human race. On the contrary, the chief business of man has been to fight evolution. He has fought it instinctively, fought it from principle, fought it with set organized purpose. He has organized institutions to prevent evolution getting away from him and going forward in spite of him. He has taught fixity and unalterability of mind to his young as the highest virtue; that is, he has taught that nonimprovement is the greatest good.

It is very important at this epochal turning point of humanity to understand how greatly the young have been deceived by their parents. This is the supreme tragedy of the human race. In no other species in the kingdom of life are the young so subject to those who produce them. In none other, because of language and the child's dependent weakness so long continued, can the parents so completely mould the mentality of their offspring. Human parents have used this strategical advantage to bar their young from learning anything new and to make them as nearly as could be mere repetitions of themselves. They have swindled their children out of the richest asset life offered to the human species. In doing so they have effectively robbed the whole of each generation of this incomparable asset, and thus from generation to generation and age to age have succeeded in depriving mankind of nearly all the superb treasures of life belonging potentially to everyone born into the cosmos.

. . . . . .

We cannot undo the past, but if we understand the past the future may be delivered from its chains, and that is the highest purpose a human being can form. Yet in this study we should not seek to overexonerate ourselves at the expense of those gone before, for what we need for our constructive task is not a small but a very great sense of our own responsibility. If we are to break the moulds that have for dreary hundreds of centuries been misshaping the human race until it culminated in our chaos, we must not fear to see these moulds as they are.

. . . . . .

[Man] should have a day for the abolition of all his beliefs. It should be an imposing day, the most memorable in all the life of mankind. By agreement mankind should then disrobe itself of the past, canceling the habitual and revered conceptions of its destiny, and giving its liberated intelligence to the consideration of all human problems in the fresh and free spirit that it would have if mind were but yesterday born. The point I aim to make is, that the brain we have is completely fettered and cross-fettered by past deposits. It is buried in fathomless débris of its own creation. But during the huge span of human existence a brain instrument of some power has gradually shaped itself. This instrument works, however, at extreme disadvantage, not unlike a man who is buried up to his neck in sand trying to walk. He has the muscles and limbs for locomotion, but is submerged in a preventive medium. The work required of man is to dig the human mind out of the accumulated sand of fossil ideas which the past ages have washed over it. The human intellect must be extricated from these mountains of thought-rubbish hardened into stone and bone before it can see light and think truth or do more than gibber foolishness and self-destruction...

...If this step is not taken—with iron courage and thoroughness, too—the promise of human survival is very small. The dead mental accumulations in man hinder him from revising the world and his own structural conduct as must be done if mankind is to live.

But the second step should accompany the first. The human brain, cleared of its decaying deposits, must think out the highest principles of constructive action, breaking away wholly from its slavery to stupidity, and make the world over on the model of these new ideas.

By these two steps the human race can survive and evolve. Without them there is little hope of its doing so.

• • • • • •

Joseph McCabe
The A B C of Evolution (1920)

The story of evolution is a great aid to correct thinking. It may begin with stars which are a long way off, but it leads to man and man's evolution. It gives you a solid scientific ground for hope and trust in man. No evolutionist can be a pessimist. The human story is only just opening. Those million years of early human development, of which I have spoken, were only the prelude. Now we know more or less where we are and what we are doing. According to the best estimates of mathematicians, man will remain on this earth for something more than ten million years yet. At the rate at which we have gone for the last hundred years, this period of time opens out a prospect of such happy developments as are beyond the capacity of the liveliest imagination. We are the factors of evolution to-day. We are the masters and the creators. Let us get the plan right and forge ahead.

• • • • • •

William Patten
The Grand Strategy of Evolution (1920)

The will and the physical power greatly to serve mankind are at hand; but the elemental intelligence, and the unity of purpose essential to constructive action, are lacking. The quickening spirit of humanity awaits the birth of its organic tabernacle.

· · · · · ·

[W]hen [the] proto-cultural age…attained its maturity, and the elements, or principles, of many separate inventions were variously combined, making them more comprehensive in their utility, serving not only one man, or one village, but many millions of human beings, for all time and all places, as the printing press, telegraph, and engine, man was unwittingly compelled, in spite of himself, to think and act constructively for all mankind.

Many factors contributed to this result, but all of them seem to have been marshalled in secret, like the different organs of a growing embryo. In the nineteenth century, to use roundly a convenient unit of time, they seem to come into cooperative action all at once, making that century the most creative period in the history of organic evolution; setting it distinctly apart as the quickening period of a world-wide, social entity; and making, at least in a physically united humanity, the philosopher's dream a reality.

We can do no more than barely outline the cultural movements of the nineteenth century, and in so doing we shall not rigidly restrict ourselves to the literal meaning of the term, for many of these movements may be traced back, historically, hundreds, or thousands, of years. But in the cases specified the movements attained well within that period a quickening momentum and a unity of action befitting the birth of a living body of world-wide dimensions.

It will best serve our present purpose, if we project these events in bold relief against the general background of organic evolution. We may then more clearly see what it was that so quickly widened man's mental horizon, increased his freedom of action, and made his organic unity a reality. The events we have in mind may be grouped as follows:

1. *The Completion of the Social Blastoderm.* With increase in population, migrations, and colonizations, man had at last, within the nineteenth century, covered all the habitable surface of the globe with a virtually continuous blastoderm,

to use an embryological term, or at least with an anastomosing network of human beings, which were everywhere within reach of one another; all of them moving more or less freely to and fro, and mingling with one another in social and reproductive intercourse...

2. *The Increment of Power.* The increase in the amount of energy at man's command...During the brief period of the nineteenth century, the resulting increase in man's constructive power, and in his power of transportation, was far greater than in all the preceding cultural eras, and is without a parallel in any animal, for any length of time whatsoever, in the whole history of evolution...

3. *The New Receptors and Perceptors...*Man alone is able to construct supplementary sense organs, or perceptors, or measurers, of external events...By means of these new physical instruments, practically all of them constructed, or greatly improved, during the nineteenth century, the precision, range, and capacity of human sense organs was magnified many hundred, thousand, or even million fold...They were building a more stable and more comprehensive register of human experience; in fact, a new social memory, and a cloud of ready witnesses that were partisans of no theory, no race, no government, and no religion...

4. *The New Ways and Means of Conveyance...*In the nineteenth century, [Man's] great trunk lines of conveyance extended completely round the earth, for the first time in evolution, definitely uniting and regulating the supplies and demands of a world-wide social life...

5. *The Orientation to a New World and the New Mental Freedom...*Evolution was, in effect, a mental emancipation

from an imaginary immutable world order. It released man from the dominion of a fixed idea, and revealed him to himself, not as the degenerate paralytic offspring of a fallen angel, the imprisoned scourge of an implacable and incompetent experimenter like himself, but as a living growing part of a living growing universe; product of the sun and soil, blood relative and next of kin to his meanest servants…Man was at last conscious of his real self; conscious of his unity with his fellow creatures, and conscious of his creative mission. He heard nature speaking to him in friendly tones, and at last realized that her gestures were not threats, but invitations to creative acts. The students and lovers of nature, walking with nature in the field, the hospital, workshop, and laboratory, were no longer, in their own estimation, or in that of their fellows, social outcasts, or harmless lunatics, or sacrilegious sorcerers and workers of witchcraft, or magic, in dens of secret iniquity, but self-respecting and respected ministers of a new order; new instruments of nature, seeking, not indeed to conquer nature, but to discover the will of nature, the better to obey it.

. . . . . .

This growth period, then, that we have had in mind was doubtless the most remarkable constructive period in the history of organic evolution. No known geological era, representing many millions of years, shows anything comparable, either in actual accomplishment, or in potential significance, with this world-wide functional unification of physical, organic, and spiritual powers.

. . . . . .

There was, and there is today, little or no consciousness of the real social significance of evolution among the most cultured peoples, or even among scientists themselves, to say nothing of the outspoken political and theological champions of the old regime. Too late for the rack and the stake, evolution was tolerated with a grimace and a joke, and became an impalpable atmosphere and an agency of intellectual compulsion. The monkey saved it from academic oblivion. All unconsciously, the basic idea in evolution took root in the popular mind, and through the agency of science and the press penetrated all social and mental strata, in countless subtle disguises; widening the general perspective, clarifying social vision, undermining ancient shams and privileges, weakening the old bonds of authority, and equalizing the power of individual men for good and evil.

• • • • • •

"Evolutionary Agencies,"
The Arbitrator, (1920)

Evolutionary Agencies

This is a catalogue of associations devoted to the alteration of unsatisfactory existing conditions—a partial list of agencies supported by forward-looking people who have visions of a better world. It is not intended to include charitable institutions which strive to mitigate suffering temporarily, nor other organizations, admirable though they be, which have for their purpose the reformation of character in the individual. The Charity Organization Society, the Salvation Army and most religious denominations are therefore excluded.

Eligibility for our catalogue is also dependent upon an altruistic and ethical purpose, a peaceful and legal method, and a reasonable prospect of success in the promotion of political and spiritual evolution. Unpopularity is no bar. The once hated abolitionists, prohibitionists, woman suffragists would rank high had not their object already been attained.

It is impossible to draw the line clearly between organizations endeavoring to promote human welfare under existing conditions and those with which we are concerned whose purpose is to remedy the defects in our established customs by changing fundamental conceptions. Therefore we must crave indulgence from those whose names have been wrongfully included, and express regrets for omission of true evolutionary agencies.

In further elucidation of the distinction between social agencies and Evolutionary Agencies, it may be pointed out that an association dedicated to work that is generally admitted by all right-minded people to be valuable has its important place but is not necessarily an Evolutionary Agency; for the beneficence of its object is granted by all and its stage of development has already been reached in evolutionary progress, so that it needs only to interest new patrons, not to convert them. Among such would be educational agencies or social service work of the churches.

The contrast may be further shown by concrete examples. The Society for the Prevention of Cruelty to Animals is admirable and represents an attitude towards the dumb creatures that is generally accepted. Its place is not here. But a society advocating for the abolition of the slaughter of animals for food would be eligible for the list, whether we agreed with its purpose or not. A society opposing race suicide would not be eligible, for the accepted idea is that the larger the population, the better for our country; but space could be given to anyone who had a reasonable theory for limitation of off-spring according to modern eugenics.

The unpopular or revolutionary proposition should not be met with set jaws and contumacious opposition, as if born of the devil, but with whatever force of argument can be mustered against it; or with enthusiastic acceptance if its morality and practicability are unanswerable, or even if it represents some advance, no matter how slight, over existing conditions.

The Arbitrator welcomes free expression by both sides concerning questions usually evaded by other publications, provided the temper is subdued, the aim ethical, and the method lawful. We wish to encourage all evolutionary agencies that are sincerely devoted to reforming human institutions, and we open our pages for the presentation of the new and radical viewpoint...It is hoped that members of the various organizations listed will be interested in following the work of the others, and will become subscribers of a paper ready to serve them all...

[The following organizations were listed]

The American Association for Labor Legislation

The American Association for International Conciliation

The American Civil Liberties Union

The American Federation of Teachers

American Medical Liberty League

The American Peace Society

The American Proportional Representation League

The American Social Hygiene Association

American Union Against Miltarism

The Citizens of the World

Clarte

The Committee of Forty-Eight

The Community Church

The Co-Operative League of America

The Esperanto Association of North America

Farmer-Labor Party

The Fellowship of Reconciliation

Free Speech League

International Free Trade League

The League of Free Nations Association

The Intercollegiate Socialist Society

The National Association for the Advancement of Colored People

The National Child Labor Committee

The National Nonpartisan League

The National Popular Government League

National Short Ballot Association

The National Voters' League

The Open Forum National Council

The Public Ownership League of America

The Rand School of Social Science

The Socialist Party of the United States

Single Tax Enclaves

Free Acres

The Voluntary Parenthood League

Woman's International League for Peace and Freedom

The Workers' Defense Union

World Peace Foundation

The Young Democracy

• • • • • •

Pierre Teilhard de Chardin
"A Note on Progress" (1920)

What is the difference between ourselves, citizens of the twentieth century, and the earliest human beings whose soul is not entirely hidden from us? In what respects may we consider ourselves their superiors and more advanced than they?

Organically speaking, the faculties of those remote forebears were probably the equal of our own. By the middle of the last Ice Age, at the latest, some human groups had attained to the expression of aesthetic powers calling for intelligence and sensibility developed to a point which we have not surpassed. To all appearance the ultimate perfection of the human *element* was achieved many thousands of years ago, which is to say that the individual instrument of thought and action may be considered to have been finalised. But there is fortunately another dimension in which variation is still possible, and in which we continue to evolve.

The great superiority over Primitive Man which we have acquired and which will be enhanced by our descendants in a degree perhaps undreamed-of by ourselves, is in the realm of self-knowledge; in our growing capacity to situate ourselves in space and time, to the point of becoming conscious of our place and responsibility in relation to the Universe.

. . . . . .

[T]his must be said, to our own honour and that of those who have toiled to make us what we are: that between the behaviour of men in the first century and our own, the difference is as great, or greater, than that between the behaviour of a fifteen-year-old boy and a man of forty. Why is this so? Because, owing to the progress of science and of thought, our actions today, whether for good or ill, proceed from an incomparably higher point of departure than those of the men who paved the way for us toward enlightenment…[T]he man of today acts in the knowledge that the choice he makes will have its repercussions through countless centuries and upon countless human beings. *He feels in himself the responsibilities and the power of an entire Universe.* Progress has not caused the *action of man* (Man himself) to change in each separate individual; but because of it the *action of human nature* (Mankind) has acquired, in every thinking man, a fulness that is wholly new.

• • • • • •

Chapman Cohen
A Grammar of Freeethought (1921)

Evolution is no more than a formula that expresses the way in which a moving balance of forces is brought about by purely mechanical means. So far as animal life is concerned this balance is expressed by the phrase "adaptation to environment." But in human society the environment is in a growing measure made up of ideas, customs, traditions, ideals, and beliefs; in a word, of factors which are themselves products of human activities. And it is for this reason that the game of civilization is very largely in our own hands. If we maintain an environment in which it is either costly or dangerous to be honest and fearless in the expression of opinion, we shall be doing our best to develop mental cowardice and hypocrisy. If we bring up the young with the successful soldier or money-maker before them as examples, while we continue to treat the scientist as a crank, and the reformer as a dangerous criminal, we shall be continuing the policy of forcing the expression of human capacity on a lower level than would otherwise be the case. If we encourage the dominance of a religion which while making a profession of disinterested loftiness continues to irradiate a narrow egotism and a pessimistic view of life, we are doing our best to perpetuate an environment which emphasizes only the poorer aspects of human motive. Two centuries of ceaseless scientific activity have taught us something of the rules of the game which we are all playing with nature whether we will or no. To-day we have a good many of the winning cards in our hands, if we will only learn to play them wisely. It is not correct to say that evolution necessarily involves progress, but it does indicate that wisdom and foresight may so control the social forces so as to turn that ceaseless change which is indicated by the law of evolution into channels that make for happiness and prosperity.

. . . . . .

[O]ne of the most striking consequences of the displacement of Christianity in the social economy...will be less time wasted on what is called philanthropic work — which is often the most harmful of all social labours — and more attention to the removal of those conditions that have made the display of philanthropy necessary. There will not be less feeling for the distressed or the unfortunate, but it will be emotion under the guidance of the intellect, and the dominant feeling will be that of indignation against the conditions that make human suffering and degradation inevitable, rather than a mere gratification of purely egoistic feeling which leaves the source of the evil untouched.

That will mean a rise in the scale of values of what one may call the intellectual virtues—the duty of truthseeking and truth speaking…[A] very high value will be placed upon the duty of investigation and the right of criticism. And one cannot easily over-estimate the consequences of a generation or two brought up in an atmosphere where such teachings obtain. It would mean a receptiveness to new ideas, a readiness to overhaul old institutions, a toleration of criticism such as would rapidly transform the whole mental atmosphere and with it enormously accentuate the capacity for, and the rapidity of, social progress.

• • • • • •

Mina Loy
"Psycho-Democracy" (1921)

Psycho-Democracy

a movement to focus human reason

on

the conscious direction of evolution

to replace the cataclysmic factor in social evolution WAR…

Psycho democracy is

Democracy of The Spirit, government by creative imagination, participation in essential wisdom—Fraternity of Intuition, the Intellect and Mother wit. (The Creator, the scholar, the natural man).

A psychological gauge applied to all social problems, for the interpretation of political, religious and financial systems.

Democratic interchange and valuation of *ideas*.

The Substitution of consciously directed evolution for revolution, *Creative inspiration for Force*, Laughter for Lethargy, Sociability for Sociology, Human psychology for Tradition.

The Psycho-Democratic Policy is

Habeas Animum.

"To illuminate the earth with her peoples eyes."

The *organization of Psycho-Democracy* is based on the laws of psychic evolution, our principles spring from Intuition, and are presented to man's intellect for maturation.

We make the experiment of a "collectivity" moved by the same intellectual logic as are the tactics of the successful individual reckoning with "actual" values and following the rules of the game of life, influencing our era by right of the merits of our (collective) personality.

Most movements have a fixed concept towards which they advance, we move away from all fixed concepts in order to advance.

. . . . . .

The Tediousness of Human Evolution is owing:

To the tendency of ideas to outlast their origin, i.e. the tendency of human institutions to outlast the psychological conditions from which they arose.

190

Psycho-Democracy considers social institutions as structural forms in collective consciousness which are subject to the same evolutional transformation as is collective consciousness itself, and that our social institutions of today will cause future generations to roar with laughter.

. . . . . .

In Psycho-Democracy shall arise men and women whose strength and originality of conception will concrete a vital ideal as the basis of International politics. This ideal which is in a nebulous state, once defined will be easier to impose on humanity than the hypnotic war lust.

For it is but logical to suppose that if the slight amount of magnetism in the make up of the world's leaders of today, is sufficient to rush great peoples on to death and agony, it will be a simple task to persuade great peoples to the effort of self realization in a life amplifying ideal; and to apply the force of reason to the solution of their life problems, which have been so acutely aggravated by the force of explosives.

And to dissuade Man from any longer considering his destiny as being extraneous to his logic.

• • • • • •

Edwin Grant Conklin
The Direction of Human Evolution (1921)

The fact that the evolution of human society and of human inventions has gone forward so rapidly that every one can see the great progress made in his own lifetime, led Samuel Butler and certain followers of his to the conclusion that social and intellectual evolution is the cause of physical evolution.

. . . . . .

The present seems to be a mutation period in the evolution of human society. One often hears the expression that certain social changes must come "by evolution or by revolution." But there is such a thing as evolution by revolution, and it seems probable that to-day we are witnessing this process in human society. Whether such evolution is going forward or backward the future only will reveal.

● ● ● ● ● ●

William Kilpatrick
"The Demand of the Times Upon Our Schools" (1921)

What is the situation confronting us? What do we see as we look over the world? The aftermath of the greatest war in history, millions upon millions killed, billions upon billions of property destroyed, new-made nations starving and quarreling as they starve, Russia in chaos, and other parts of the world little better off. Everywhere international suspicions, fears, selfishness, and, in too many cases, despair. If we look into the domestic affairs of our country, we find a like welter of unrest, strikes, threats, bitter partisanship, industrial warfare, class hatreds. Wherever we look, at home or abroad, the future seems dark.

But let us look beneath the surface of this most discouraging situation, and see if more deeply moving tendencies may not furnish guidance. What is the characteristic feature of the period in which we live? Is there anything to distinguish it from preceding periods? The answer seems clear: our generation is distinguished by the growth of tested thought, and its application to the affairs of men. Other periods have thought, and thought acutely, but the characteristic features of our time are found in the tendency to test suggested thought in as objective a fashion as possible, in the accumulation of thought so tested, and in the disposition to apply this thought to improving the affairs of men.

Three far-reaching tendencies co-exist with this modern characteristic and receive greatly added impetus from it; namely, a tendency to criticize our social institutions, a tendency toward the aggregation of men in larger and larger units and their integration in ever closer relationships, and a democratic tendency. It is not suggested that criticism is a modern phenomenon...What is claimed is that modern criticism finds its chief support in the growth and application of tested thought...We may confidently expect a stronger and more penetrating criticism to make a yet more inclusive scrutiny of human institutions and a yet more radical tendency to change things in accordance with criticism. Whether we approve or not, whether it be a Frankenstein or not, the spirit of criticism is loose in the modern world.

...The second tendency is toward the aggregation of men in ever growing units and the integration of mankind in ever more numerous relationships...As never before, we are members of one society. The evening speech of a prime minister is read by the whole world the next morning. A murder in southern Europe involves the whole world in war. A crop failure in a remote corner of the world threatens hunger for the poor of Europe. More and larger aggregations, closer and more numerous integrations; the entire world hangs closer together as a whole in a degree never known before. And again the end is not in sight. The process is endless unless civilization begins to die.

The third tendency, that toward democracy, is not so easy to either to define or to explain, but its forward sweep cannot be questioned...And still again the end is not in sight; democracy will not stay its stride till many matters be set straight. Nor will the end then come, for it is an infinite world in which we live, and the spirit of human justice will ever find work lying at its hand.

As these three great social tendencies have received strength and impetus from the growth and application of tested thought, so do all, working together in their turn, lead to two conclusions especially significant for us.

The first is that authoritarianism in the affairs of men wanes to its death...More significant, if possible, is the second conclusion...namely, that change is inherent in the very process of civilization, and, so far as it concerns human institutions, practically all embracing. It is only too true that many among us have been hoping and praying that affairs will at last quiet down and let civilization catch its breath...[T]aking centuries together, change will never cease. On the contrary it will almost certainly become increasingly rapid...Every first class invention makes far-reaching demands for changes in human behavior and relationships. The increasing aggregation of human affairs hastens the spread of change. More first class inventions have been made in the past two hundred years than in the two thousand years before...The only thing we can assert with certainty is that we face rapidly changing forces which are shaping an unknown future.

. . . . . .

Change is inevitable but progress is contingent. It is, then, exceedingly important that the rising generation believe in orderly processes of capitalizing change rather than in violent and catastrophic measures. The road to revolution, if often traveled, can but lead to the death of civilization.

As the world faces many great and unknown changes it is possible that we, by taking thought, can prepare our youth specifically to meet that unknown situation. We must prepare them to adapt themselves, when the time shall come, to that unknown and shifting world. We must then, as far as we can, make our young people adaptable, capable of easy and intelligent adjustment. It is methods of investigation they must be taught, not specific solutions. That they shall think and not what they shall think must be our aim.

. . . . . .

The school we have inherited has come down to us from a remote past when education was mainly designed on the one hand to inculcate docility and on the other to impart bare knowledge or skill. These things no longer satisfy. The duty of the school is now as large as is the life of the child who is to live in the democratic society of the future. It is our part to see that the ideals and attitudes necessary for that democratic life enter into the very innermost souls of our young people. In no other way can we meet the demand of the times upon our schools. In preparation for that unknown and changing future, books and examinations are not sufficient. Ideals and attitudes are immensely more important. Among these, three ideals especially stand out as worthy of our every endeavor, unselfishness, adaptability, responsibility.

• • • • • •

Hendrick van Loon
The Story of Mankind (1921)

We modern men and women are not "modern" at all. On
the contrary we still belong to the last generations of the
cave-dwellers. The foundation for a new era was laid but
yesterday. The human race was given its first chance to
become truly civilised when it took courage to question all
things and made "knowledge and understanding" the
foundation upon which to create a more reasonable and
sensible society of human beings. The Great War was the
"growing-pain" of this new world.

For a long time to come people will write mighty books
to prove that this or that or the other person brought about
the war...The original mistake, which was responsible for
all this misery, was committed when our scientists began to
create a new world of steel and iron and chemistry and
electricity and forgot that the human mind is slower than
the proverbial turtle, is lazier than the well-known sloth,
and marches from one hundred to three hundred years
behind the small group of courageous leaders.

A Zulu in a frock coat is still a Zulu. A dog trained to
ride a bicycle and smoke a pipe is still a dog. And a human
being with the mind of a sixteenth century tradesman
driving a 1921 Rolls-Royce is still a human being with the
mind of a sixteenth century tradesman.

• • • • • •

The Ship of State, (that old and trusted expression which is
ever new and always picturesque,) of the Egyptians and the
Greeks and the Romans and the Venetians and the

merchant adventurers of the seventeenth century had been a sturdy craft, constructed of well-seasoned wood, and commanded by officers who knew both their crew and their vessel and who understood the limitations of the art of navigating which had been handed down to them by their ancestors.

Then came the new age of iron and steel and machinery. First one part, then another of the old ship of state was changed. Her dimensions were increased. The sails were discarded for steam. Better living quarters were established, but more people were forced to go down into the stoke-hole, and while the work was safe and fairly remunerative, they did not like it as well as their old and more dangerous job in the rigging. Finally, and almost imperceptibly, the old wooden square-rigger had been transformed into a modern ocean liner. But the captain and the mates remained the same. They were appointed or elected in the same way as a hundred years before. They were taught the same system of navigation which had served the mariners of the fifteenth century. In their cabins hung the same charts and signal flags which had done service in the days of Louis XIV and Frederick the Great. In short, they were (through no fault of their own) completely incompetent...

[T]he moral of the story is a simple one. The world is in dreadful need of men who will assume the new leadership who will have the courage of their own visions and who will recognise clearly that we are only at the beginning of the voyage, and have to learn an entirely new system of seamanship.

• • • • • •

H.G. Wells

"An Apology for a World Utopia" (1921)

What is a Utopia? It is a first sketch plan of a prepared replacement or change in human institutions. If a man is going to build a house the first thing he does is to make a sketch plan of the house he is going to build...We find a constant use of the word Utopian in contrast to the word practical. There is a certain type of man who, when you talk about a Utopia, leans back at once prepared to smile. Part of that smiling, if I may say so, is sheer stupidity; it is due to the inability to conceive such a thing as change...But there is also another reason in addition to the general inability to imagine change at all why Utopias are regarded as impracticable. It is because they have been so frequently presented as impracticable propositions...and there has been a general tendency to represent the states as occurring in some distant island, or some remote part of the earth. Why is that? The reason is not far to seek. Technically every Utopia is a treason to the thing that is. It is also usually a slight to the people who are.

. . . . . .

What our western political and social life suffers from is that limitation of vision that makes men prefer short views, and immediate issues...Who do I mean by people of short views? I mean the statesman, the politicians, and the leading people of our times. And what do I mean by people of short views? I mean, to be plain, people imperfectly educated so that they do not see life as a whole, nor the problems of life as related in any intelligible way one to another or to any general scheme. They take the road before them because it is the road before them, and they do not ask where it leads: they are methodically short-sighted, and they take a sort of pride in being short-sighted, as though there is something eminently practical in a restricted vision. They accept transitory conditions as though they were permanent conditions, and build on dry sand as though they built on rocks, heedless that sooner or later a storm must inevitably wash their foundations away.

[S]hort views work very well in settled times…[S]uddenly came the great catastrophe of the war, and found our politicians and statesman entirely inadequate…In the place of party issues they were faced with world issues. They had no vision, no Utopia to guide them.

. . . . . .

There is one fundamental idea upon which I am working: that this world is face to face with, and has to adapt itself to, a change of conditions unprecedented in history, and that the realization of the Utopia of the World State is the only possible way of making that adaptation. What is this change of conditions? It is that there has been a complete alteration in the range of human activities through the development of new and rapid means of communication during the past hundred years.

. . . . . .

Is there any precedent to justify us in hoping that such a change in world ideas is possible? I think there is…In the past there have been very great changes in human thought…[I]f you will consider the spread of…very complex and difficult religions, and compare the means at the disposal of their promotors with the means at the disposal of intelligent people to-day, you will find many reasons for believing that a recasting of people's ideas throughout the world and into the framework of a universal state is by no means an impossible project...Now, to-day, we have means of putting ideas and arguments swiftly and effectively before people all over the world at the same time, such as no one could have dreamt of a hundred years ago.

• • • • • •

William F. Ogburn
Social Change with Respect to Culture and Original Nature
(1922)

Many of the facts of life and of history are in harmony with the theories of the repression from consciousness of the unpleasant...A person may find it distinctly satisfying to recall some painful event, if by recalling it he can prevent a repetition in the future. In other words, when there is a way out, an appreciated knowledge gained by experience or a prospect of improvement, the unpleasant events of the past are not so unpleasant to remember. And so it would seem that if there is a prospect of improvement in social conditions, something to be gained by avoiding a repetition of these objectionable situations, the past may be less glorified and past conditions may be seen more nearly as they were. In a rapidly changing culture, individuals identify themselves with these changes, work with hope for improvement and the concept of "better times" may tend to replace the notion of "the good old days."

. . . . . .

The thesis is that the various parts of modern culture are not changing at the same rate, some parts are changing much more rapidly than others; and that since there is a correlation and interdependence of parts, a rapid change in one part of our culture requires readjustments through other changes in the various correlated parts of culture...Where one part of culture changes first, through some discovery or invention, and occasions changes in some part of culture dependent upon it, there frequently is a delay in the changes occasioned in the dependent part of culture. The extent of this lag will vary according to the nature of the cultural material, but may exist for a considerable number of years, during which time there may be said to be a maladjustment. It is desirable to reduce the period of maladjustment, to make the cultural adjustments as quickly as possible.

. . . . . .

[T]hinking in terms of an ideal, the adaptive culture is never wholly harmoniously adapted to the material conditions, for the reason that there is no ideal limit to this harmonious relationship. For instance, workmen's compensations, or feminism, or conservation of forests, may be more satisfactory than former mores, but who shall say that these adjustments are ideal? When we can think of better adjustments, that is, when we make inventions in the adaptive culture, the old adaptive culture will appear to lag, since it will take, in a purely physical way, some time for an invention to spread or be adapted, even after it has been thought out or applied once.

. . . . . .

[T]he phenomenon of [cultural] lag would be found only in a situation of cultural change. Since it is in recent times that cultural changes are so frequent, the lags in adaptive culture are expected to be a problem of only modern times...Since lags in social movements causing social maladjustments follow changes in material culture, and since there are many rapid changes in material culture, it follows that there will be an accumulation of these lags and maladjustments...Such a development creates quite a task for those who would direct the course of social progress, the task of eliminating these maladjustments by making the adjustments to material changes more rapid.

. . . . . .

While it is true that the changes occurring today are preponderantly in the culture rather than in biological man, it does not follow that these changes are controlled and purposively directed by man. Despite the fact that man appears as an active agent in these changes, cultural factors such as social forces and economic processes play quite a determining part in these changes. It is not true that man creates culture freely as he wills. The extent to which man is a freely determining agent in directing social evolution is one of the fundamental questions in sociology.

. . . . . .

[T]here is evidence of a lack of harmonious adjustment between modern culture and human nature, as seen particularly in the extent of neuroses and functional psychoses, and in certain social problems. In the more acute cases of maladjustment the more probable solution of the difficulty lies not in attempts to change human nature but rather in attempts to change culture; for the reason that in such acute instances further efforts at changing human nature result in repression of instincts which is followed by objectionable consequences to the individual and aggravations of the social problems. On the other hand, the nature of cultural growth and change shows that it is futile to plan any wholesale and powerful control of the course of social evolution. Directing the change of culture is much more difficult than is customarily conceived. It is, however, not necessary to change culture as a whole, for relatively minor changes may result in much better adjustments. These changes, though difficult, may be looked forward to as feasible, if not now, certainly in time. They concern influences affecting the life of children and parental affection, sex education, modification of social codes, shorter hours of labor, recognition of boundaries to selfishness, specific social programmes, and finally it is thought that possibilities of better adjustment lie in the wise development of substitutive activities such as recreation.

• • • • • •

John M. Mecklin
An Introduction to Social Ethics (1922)

As a nation we have to a large extent accepted the dualism between the ideal and the factual present in the beginnings of national life as part of the eternal order of things. We have not yet felt the imperative necessity of uniting the two. This has resulted in a gradual triumph of the factual for the simple reason that it is ever with us. We are never able to escape entirely from the disciplinary effects of the brute facts as they impinge upon us from every angle of experience. They inevitably shape us to their will unless we are able to surmount them or make them instruments for the attainment of a more abundant life through the ideal. Perhaps it was asking too much of America to refine and spiritualize the crude ore as she dug it from the mine. But it remains true, nevertheless, that without some such process of refinement we shall never be able to distinguish the dross from the gold. The day is already far spent when we can justify our neglect of the duty critically to weigh and evaluate on the ground of the urgent call of the practical. The gap between the ideal and the actual must be closed. The confusions and contradictions in our highest ideals must be remedied in the interest of a sane and progressive national life.

. . . . . .

The machine, more than any one factor, determines the daily routine of our lives...The machine has, in fact, transformed, within the last two or three generations, the very structure and spirit of our civilization...Why do we love the tool and fear the machine? The answer is that the tool is the servant of the human will and in the case of the artist or skilled worker is almost a part of himself and breathes his own rational and creative genius. The machine, on the other hand, is independent of the will, self-sufficient, indifferent. It works with rhythmic, deadly, predestined accuracy. It is the grinning skeleton of a self that is utterly without a soul. It has the precision, the logical sequence, the coordination and finality of reason but is devoid of conscience. When, therefore, the machine closes in upon us and seeks to subject us to its economy the very essence of personality is threatened, namely, the free, creative, moral will. We fear the machine, therefore, because when it seeks to rule it becomes a moral monstrosity.

To surrender to the machine process, therefore, is to negate all those values that make human life worth while. The horror of German militarism lay in the mechanizing of an entire civilization. It was the spectacle of a great people organized with all the effectiveness of a skilfully articulated machine and yet actuated by the conscience of a mob that filled the world with a nameless horror. For here was a transvaluation of values that seemed to change our hard won paradise into a hell. Mankind had been taught to associate the achievements of science with the darling aspirations of the race. Now men beheld to their dismay the devil masquerading in the apparel of an angel of light. The disillusionment was a terrible one but it has brought much searching of the heart. It has taught us that the machine process can only be of value as it is made to serve and not to rule the spirit of man.

. . . . . .

The philosophy of the machine is most clearly in evidence in that phase of the industrial world for which it is chiefly responsible, namely, in the modern large corporation. The materialism, the impersonal selfishness, the heartless exercise of power, the cold and unscrupulous rationalism that has made the term "big business" anathema in the minds of many good people is to be explained by the fact that the large-scale business of to-day still to a large extent reflects the spirit of the machine process of which it is but the creature. The influence of the machine is in evidence in the impersonality of society. The machine is assuming more and more of those services that men once performed for each other. The telephone, the telegraph and the printing press have depersonalized our social contacts. Even the people on a crowded street-car hurrying to their places of business are wrapped in an atmosphere of impersonal remoteness. This impersonality made possible by the machine saves time and energy, to be sure, but at the sacrifice of the social and moral discipline gained through entering sympathetically and intelligently into the lives of our fellows. It makes the problem of securing democratic like-mindedness increasingly difficult.

Corresponding to the impersonality of the Great Society demanded by the machine we have the impersonality of the money-economy. In the rapid whirl of our modern industrial order, with its multifarious mechanical standardizations and its utter indifference to those values represented by ethics, religion and democracy, the machine process when allowed free play, works like a powerful acid to disintegrate the tissues of the social organism. It is not only impersonal but it favors a sort of mechanical atomism...Because of this impersonal and mechanical atomism peculiar to the machine process it becomes imperatively necessary to have some universal arbiter of values, a common denominator to which these various standardizations of the machine process can be reduced. The dollar coordinates the mechanical units of the machine process and saves us from chaos. Yet the dollar partakes of the impersonality of these units. The pecuniary impersonalism of the dollar, therefore, is the correlative of the mechanical impersonalism of the machine process.

It is in scientific management, however, that the last refinements of the machine process appear. In it we find expressed the quintessence of the spirit of the machine...In the claims of scientific management stand revealed all the weaknesses inherent in the philosophy of the machine. It fails to distinguish the mechanical and material from the purely human.

. . . . . .

[Paraphrasing Thornstein Veblen] [W]hile discrediting ancient loyalties in ethics and religion the machine offers us no constructive program for the future; it forces men to think in terms of the opaque, unteleological and unmoral principles of mechanical causation.

. . . . . .

The machine process in and of itself has infinite potentialities for human betterment. But to seek in the principle of physical causation upon which it is built the measure of values for its use and the philosophy that is to provide us with the driving force of society is grievous injustice to the machine process itself. The trellis that bears the vine may be coherent and logically articulated but in and of itself is dead, inert, a gaunt and unlovely skeleton. When its firm and logical framework has been appropriated by the vine it becomes eloquent with the beauty and freshness of an expanding organism. Its mechanical form is gathered up into the higher life of the vine and gains a new significance because it serves this higher life. Much in the same way must we conceive of the function of the vast mechanical frame work of the machine process in the social organism. It is here to serve, not to rule the life of man.

● ● ● ● ● ●

Joseph Fort Newton
"Salvation by Education" (1922)

Three forces will shape the future of our humanity, the democratic principle, the spirit of science and the light and power of an emancipated religion. These three forces must work together, if we are to escape a conservatism without sympathy, a radicalism without sense, and a future without disaster. Democracy is inevitable. Nothing can stop it.

Industry, no less than politics, must yield to its sway. But democracy is not enough. It is only the raw truth and fact about life—fluid, plastic, prophetic—waiting to be wrought into shapes of usefulness and beauty. Unless an inevitable democracy can be enlightened by science and evangelized by spiritual faith, the future will be drab and dingy. Massed ignorance does not make wisdom. Truth is not revealed by the counting of noses. Long ago Lowell said that "democracy is an experiment," and the experiment is not yet complete. Without moral idealism, without spiritual leadership, without practical fraternity, democracy will fail.

• • • • • •

L.L. Bernard
"The Conditions of Social Progress" (1922)

[T]o make certain that the future interests of mankind shall triumph over the merely immediate, when they conflict, that social progress as well as social welfare shall be promoted, is a…difficult task. People do not easily tie up their affections with a vaguely perceived and impersonal future. They live mainly in the present. To secure a proper regard for the interests of social progress it is necessary to make people live in the future also…A growth of knowledge of the social sciences, especially of theories of social progress and their general dissemination, should project the sympathetic understandings of men farther into the future and tend to identify them in some measure with it. Such an understanding must ultimately and inevitably carry over into the execution of certain programs, necessary even for the present generation, such as the practice of conservation, the construction of public works, warfare against disease, the dissemination of certain kinds of knowledge, the control of unrestrained action by men and states, leading possibly to warfare or other forms of anti-social exploitation. These undertakings may often serve to connect, in the minds of their promoters, the interests of the future generations with those of the present, thus leading to the planning of inclusive programs to cover the needs of as many generations as possible.

. . . . . .

Modern social life has become increasingly complex and the increase in this direction shows no abatement. We have a hundred social problems to solve where our great grandfathers had one or none. The very process of earning a livelihood has become complicated with an infinite number of details of scientific and mechanical technique, with markets and marketing, the problems of credit and exchange, business and government, and the like. A score, a hundred, a thousand problems of health and sanitation have arisen where formerly was only the bliss of ignorance. The very technique of living, of mastering and enjoying the comforts of life, the volume of social intercourse, the richness of opportunity for amusement, all these and scores of other things oppress us and steal from us the leisure for creative work and time for rest and recuperation. They drive us irresistibly toward the accumulation of more income with which to satisfy ever new and increasing demands. We are unable to detach ourselves from the details of life long enough to grasp its meaning and to plan for social progress. If we are to withstand the strain of this process and be effective in the struggle for social improvement we must either find some method of mastering the complexity of life or invent a formula or formulae for its simplification. Apparently we cannot look for a mutation of our nervous systems which will enable us to handle more details with less nervous strain. Hence our greatest hope would seem to lie in the direction of a better selection of the details of living which we find worth while and the better organization of these into an administrative whole.

. . . . . .

While social progress would not be impossible without a system of universal and profound education, it would be greatly facilitated by rendering all people self-directive through a full knowledge of the world and society in which they live.

• • • • • •

Carl Emil Seashore
Address to the American Peace Society (1922)

While conscious of the heavy war clouds hanging over us, speaking as a psychologist, I should like to say a few cheerful things with reference to the future of peace. In the first place, the evolution of human society and its resources is going to be from now on a *consciously directed* evolution. We are right in the heart of the transition, breaking away from what might be called mere natural selection and traditional sway. Until recently, progressive people have acted like squatters taking possession of undeveloped resources as they found them. In politics, religion, and art there has been but little generalization. Cults, sects, and schools have struggled for survival as primitive savage tribes struggled for bodily supremacy. Health has been regarded as a gift and disease as a matter of fate, both in an unjustifiable sense. We are just emerging from a provincial type of government, primitive industry, and a dead philosophy.

Witness before us consciously directed movements for the conservation of natural resources—physical and mental, organic and inorganic, human and animal, individual and national. The care of health of body and mind, which was until recently an individual affair, is now a state and social affair, organized on principles of society and government. Eugenics, the science or art of improving offspring, especially of the human race, and euthenics, the science of improving the human race by external influences, apart from considerations of heredity, are making tremendous strides and will shape the future of man. The League of Nations, peace conferences—world movements in every direction—are consciously directing the course of evolution. Birth control and race suicide are made the objects of conscious deliberation. The educational unit is a world unit.

Contrast this conscious direction of enormously rapid development in every phase of human life and endeavor with the blind march of chance and tradition before the present century. Now, conscious direction means deliberation. Deliberation means a second thought and the approval of reason. The universal sway of conscious direction of evolution will inevitably be in the direction of world peace.

In the second place, *man is getting better*. Opposing evolution, Bryan and his following maintain that man was created in a perfect state and has degenerated; and the ultra-evolutionists maintain that the civilization of the five most cultured nations of the world is on the verge of decline. Yet I say man is getting better. What is the evidence? One line of evidence is found in the principle that a civilization can be measured in terms of the number of people who can live together in peace. Among the most primitive people this is less than thirty; and, as culture gradually comes in, the unit gets larger and larger until, under the stars and stripes, a hundred million people can dwell together in the bonds of peace. This increase in the size of the political unit has been a gradually progressive one from the most primitive times; and no one can seriously question the probability of its culmination in civilization as a world unit.

But look at it from another point of view. Is man getting better? Trace the evolution or history of marriage and chastity in the family; trace the evolution of the status of woman; trace the evolution of the treatment of the sick and wounded, particularly the insane; trace the evolution of forethought for health and morals; trace each of these from its very inception and no one can imagine that the steady progress of advance should stop suddenly at this moment. Evil is never on a straight line. It proceeds in whirling vortices. So, on the basis of the past, we rejoice that man is growing better, and that the rate of improvement is improving in geometric ratio.

In the third place, man is *adaptable*. Within the last decade countless theorists have held that human nature is so thoroughly established that a few hundred years of culture has not modified human nature seriously and will never do so. They are right. There are always countless processes of death and decay in the upward trend of life. It is a fact that we have been thousands of millions of years in the making and human nature is not altered fundamentally by a few hundred years of culture or environment. But the fortunate fact is that human nature, even in its lowest form, is endowed with almost limitless resources, so that, given the opportunity for cultural expression and refinement, the individual will be better from generation to generation, as he creates a better environment. The education and enfranchisement of women will make the world different; perhaps not in immediate political reaction, but in the long process of evolution. Political forethought by both men and women will make the world better.

It is trite to say that environment is opportunity. Given a consciously directed environment, and original man will be found amply responsive for adapting himself without suddenly changing human nature appreciably.

In the last place, the world is getting smaller. The development of the means of communication and travel, of transmission of information, the stock of common knowledge, the mingling of races in finance, industries, and art annihilates distance and boundaries and tends to make the world one. When nations in the most distant parts of the earth can daily see and hear one another through moving pictures and radio broadcast, they will become neighbors.

• • • • • •

L.L. Bernard
"Invention and Social Progress" (1923)

The greatest advances in the future will probably come through the application of method inventions in the social sciences to the improvement of our social institutions and organization. Our social organization now lags behind our physical achievements. This is due in part to the fact that the social sciences are not so well developed as the physical sciences and consequently dependable and workable method inventions are not so easily produced in these sciences. But our failure adequately to apply science to the perfection of social organization is also in large measure due to the opposition of prejudice, ignorance, and self-interest to interference with the old social order to which men have become adjusted.

. . . . . .

Human society—at least our section of it in the West—is becoming conscious of itself. It no longer muddles along merely as blindly selective social evolution. Our social evolution is becoming in a measure socially self-conscious and socially self-directive. This is indicated not alone by the existence of numerous forums for public discussion and journals of opinion, but also by the recent rapid development of the social sciences and of a very extensive literature in these sciences. Man is busily engaged in studying his society in various aspects—economic, political, religious, ethical, humanitarian, etc.—and in attempting to invent more adequately adapted institutional forms for the carrying on of an intelligent and economically or efficiently organized social life. Inventions are becoming increasingly purposive and projective.

. . . . . .

[T]he types of inventions which are most urgently needed in these various fields are distinctly projective in character. Empirical invention will not meet the demands of consciously directed social progress in the future. We have reached the stage in social development where we must make rapid strides and long leaps.

. . . . . .

Robert Sterling Yard

"The Place of Our National Parks in Education" (1923)

Absurdly, it is the practice to speak of Nature, meaning the earth, the things which grow out of it and the creatures which live upon it, as something quite distinct from man. But one cannot separate man from his producing and supporting environment. He is part and parcel of the earth, a stage in its history, to which his contribution is a mind enough higher than its predecessors' to perceive, faintly, the spiritual. He is an episode in an evolution which began "When God created the Heaven and the Earth." He is kin to the granite, the pine, and the ape.

. . . . . .

Inevitably, out of the enthusiastic study of nature has grown the desire to protect and preserve…Conservation of nature's riches for the material profit of the future had long been advocated and is increasingly practiced. But the word conservation has recently acquired another meaning far different from utility. Late, but not too late, we recognize man uneducated as the destroyer for gain, and conceive of man educated as the preserver of what remains and the builder thereupon of unimaginable products of mind…We should have a separate word for this newer and greater meaning of Conservation, this preservation of nature for preservation's sake. The idea is latent in every human mind.

. . . . . .

Albert P. Weiss
"The Aims of Social Evolution" (1923)

The aim of social evolution as a cosmical process is that of producing larger and more complex electron-proton aggregates, but as a human process, the aim of social evolution is that of developing a social organization that will yield for each individual a maximum of individualization with a minimum of standardization.

• • • • • •

Clark Wissler
Man and Culture (1923)

The thing we are now striving for is the rationalization of the culture function as a whole...the great World War of our day has hastened the event by turning the eyes of all to culture. Even the term culture soon found its way into the average vocabulary, thus furnishing the basis for a serious inquiry into the nature of the phenomenon.

. . . . . .

[W]e may expect eventually a people who handle their culture just as effectually as the most enlightened of us do sanitation, diet, etc. We may surely expect this, because such a trend has so far marked the whole range of culture history and nothing short of a complete reversal of the process can prevent it.

. . . . . .

Our ideal aims at a condition that will give each man or woman the fullest measure of culture. In consequence, it is of the greatest moment that we arrive at a knowledge of

216

how culture moves, and it is the application of this knowledge which we here speak of as rationalization. So to take a rationalistic attitude toward culture, one must first become fully aware of its existence, and seek to understand its processes. Then with each advance in such knowledge will come increased control. Yet in no case are we to expect that man's original nature will cease to function and be displaced by an age of pure reason. The rationalization we have in mind is increasing direction and control of native behavior, and not its abolition. In other words, when man comes into even a partial understanding of what culture is, he will have achieved another advance in reflective thinking, and thence begin to manipulate, not merely isolated individual behavior, but group behavior.

· · · · · ·

It was an easy step from the realization of the individual to the conception of society and to the assumption that society itself could be rationalized and directed. Such a consciousness of ourselves functioning as a group is coincident with the rise of sociology as an academic subject, and whereas a century or more ago men were thinking in terms of the individual, they came during the last half century to see themselves in society.

· · · · · ·

[W]e have seen how our people are just becoming conscious of the existence of culture and of themselves as participating in culture. So while we have attained social consciousness or the conception of a self-realized society, into culture consciousness we are just now groping our way.

· · · · · ·

[T]here has been in Euro-American culture a marvelous speeding up, due, in the main, to reflections and manipulations with these methods of ameliorating the common lot of men. And now, at last, is coming the consciousness that we have a culture which follows laws and conditions, all of which can be discovered and actions of peoples manipulated to further speed the progress...What the future has in store for us we can but guess. The most obvious fact of all is the progressive acceleration in the triumphant progress of this further rationalization of culture traits. To what speed yet it may attain! If there be those who have misgivings as to whether the nervous system can stand the strain, think kindly of them, for they may be the advance guards of another triumph in reflective thinking.

• • • • • •

Francis Marion Rust
The Evolution of Democracy (1923)

Material invention and highly developed general intelligence of the masses is rapidly overcoming time and space in their ordinary relation to mankind, thus making imperative a general government for the world. The League of Nations is an effort in the right direction.

• • • • • •

F.S. Marvin
Science and Civilization (1923)

About the middle of the last century several great thinkers had combined their voices in proclaiming the historical authenticity and future certainty of progress. Darwin followed shortly after and seemed to give a biological guarantee. The sixty years that have followed have by no means disposed either of Darwin or of a doctrine of general progress, but they have induced a more critical frame of mind. We ask now, 'In what does progress consist, and what grounds are there to believe that it will continue?' just as in the case of Darwin the biologists have inquired 'What is a variation, and how can we imagine certain variations to occur which seem so miraculously favourable to the needs of the creature?' Such questionings as these have during the last few decades covered all the ground of the great synthetic thinkers of the early nineteenth century. Then came the War. It seemed to extinguish the hopes of assured progress and speedy peace and happiness for all mankind which first shone out at the end of the eighteenth century and irradiated the century which followed.

Both the accession of criticism and the wave of pessimism were natural, but not final. It was healthy to subject the wide and glowing generalizations of Condorcet or of Comte to close examination, but it would be absurd to dismiss a widely grounded conclusion as to the growth of human society because some of its discoverers and exponents have expressed it in too unqualified a way. The growth of human society being the most extensive and complex example of evolution, the widest and longest views are needed to compass it to any purpose.

. . . . . .

Th[e] growing complexity of human problems, without a corresponding growth of the human brain to deal with them, is perhaps the most serious obstacle which faces the onward march of mankind. It is exemplified equally on the theoretical and the practical field. The realm of science is now so vast that a small subdivision of one of its branches is enough to occupy the lifelong energies of a devoted student who, even a hundred years ago, might have hoped to acquire a competent acquaintance with the whole. And in the practical sphere the affairs of one region, which to the ancients seemed to embrace the world, are now in one department of the British Foreign Office, itself one member of the League of Nations. We need not despair of the human intellect: its material organ, the brain, has demonstrably developed since prehistoric times. But the spiritual organ which must grapple with the problems of the future will not be located in any one cranium: it will be the co-operative working of many minds...To render such co-operation as effective as possible, to make the collective mind function with something of the quickness and the decision of a good individual, is the highest problem of organization.

Such is the necessary method both for social studies and for social action in the modern world, but a general theory and spirit are also needed to give a moving force to the machine. Mount Everest could not be climbed without a conviction of its possibility and a hopeful determination to do it. This is given in the social sphere by the general theory of progress, based on the nature of man and the known broad facts of history. He has advanced from a lower to a higher state of existence, for we cannot believe that his recently acquired consciousness and study of this

220

advance will operate as a brake to its further continuance. Man had been gaining science for uncounted ages before he became a conscious philosopher. Since he began to work at science consciously, the growth has been immeasurably greater. We may expect the same result to follow man's awakening to progress. The progress was a fact long ages before it was detected and its outlines described in a ' law '. The theorizing will not destroy the movement but accelerate its rate. The sadness of to-day and yesterday is but a trough between the great advancing waves, the reaction against a doctrine announced perhaps too loudly and with too little qualification by the earlier prophets.

• • • • • •

Marvin L. Darsie
"The Spiritual in Education" (1924)

[T]here can be no progress without see-ers of visions and dreamers of dreams. Conscious social evolution consists in imagining a better world, and then striving to realize it in the sphere of action...A progressive people, a spiritually virile people, must be trained to live in art [sic] in a world of constructive dreaming.

• • • • • •

Joseph K. Hart
The Discovery of Intelligence (1924)

[U]ntil the nineteenth century no satisfactory theory of revolt or change had been made, despite the fact that many revolutions had occurred and many changes had taken place. Men did things under the pressure of events which no theory or philosophy had been able to justify. Innovators like Socrates, Jesus, Martin Luther, and Rousseau, while they expressed the *hopes* of mankind, in opposition to the stagnation of the folkways, had difficulty in justifying their conduct on rational grounds. But in the nineteenth century all these reconstructive movements and hopes of the past found justification in the theory of evolution.

. . . . . .

History comes to a new climax; a new theory of the nature of the world, of human life and experience, is set forth—a theory that in dignity and significance is worthy to take its place alongside medievalism and to contend with that theory for the allegiance of men. History becomes aware of its own movements and its own inner workings; it justifies its restless past. Henceforth it will be avowedly and intentionally evolutionary in its ideals and its modes. Moreover, for the future, history may be studied in the hope that the race will learn how to make history; and thus the processes of making history will in the future be somewhat under the control of human intention.

. . . . . .

All institutions are tools by which man has gained, and will continue to regain, control over the conditions in which he lives. All institutions are, therefore, subject to the reconstructive needs of experience. This includes the school...That education which was developed to meet a certain social need in a certain past age may well fail in another age under changed conditions. But schools, like all institutions, are conservative. They tend to maintain their old functions long after their service has ended, because, dealing with old informations, as they do so largely, they do not always recognize when their work has ceased to be vital...Schools may even accept the general theory of evolution and teach it, while retaining obstructive survivals of old social methods which, under changed conditions, offer no convincing reason for existence.

• • • • • •

Carolyn MacDonald
Letter to the Editor, *The Forum* (1924)

The enfranchisement of women is only a step in earthly evolution. Earthly evolution is only a phase in the evolution of the universe.

• • • • • •

J. Arthur Thomson
What is Man (1924)

Critics point out that many a big change in mankind, like industrialism, has probably done as much harm as good; that many changes have been very miserable at the time and of dubious benefit when effected. We look round and see disease, bad health, low vitality, dullness, insufficient food, slums, miserable houses, disharmonious domestic life, unemployment, unhappiness at work, boredom at leisure, and how much more that does not seem consistent with progress. We must, therefore, add to our definition. Progress must include *social* integration; it must include *more* chance for all to share in it. Our definition broadens. Progress is a balanced movement of a social whole towards the fuller embodiment of the supreme values, and at the same time a more all-round realization of the physical and biological pre-conditions, namely, the wealth and health which secure stability.

There seems value in recognizing the pre-conditions — wealth and health — as fundamental to the supreme values. Not that seeking them *first* is necessarily always right…A new heart, before a new earth; so Eupsychics — good education may be the shortest way to Eutopia, or good environment…

Yet there is sound sense in emphasizing that a fuller realization of the supreme values will not be stable or all-round unless there is a general sharing in good health (in a high sense) and sufficient wealth (i.e., adequate command of energy) to allow of some leisure and enjoyment…

Vigour is a Eugenic ideal; but a vigorous serf is not a human ideal; nor is vigour in an ugly place a satisfactory result. A beautiful countryside or a beautiful city is a Eutopian ideal, but it is not a human ideal if the people are all toiling and moiling unrelieved by joy. Wholesome occupation is a Eutechnic ideal, but it fails of human completeness unless the workers have good health and pleasant homes. Progress is not one thing, but many. It is imperfect in proportion to its particulateness.

. . . . . .

Without postulating mutations on a big scale in hereditary "Nature," we see endless possibilities of progressive change by ameliorations in "Nurture." There is no end to what can be done in improving all the surrounding influences that play upon the individual — for that is what *nurture* means; and though the individual's gains may not be entailable, they tend to be registered in the social heritage. There they form an atmosphere or soil in which new constitutional variations in the right direction have a good chance to flourish, and these are transmissible. Moreover, the external heritage forms, in proportion as it is enriched, a safeguard against man's slipping down the rungs of the steep ladder of evolution. This, indeed, is one of the central secrets of progress.

. . . . . .

Mathematicians speak of an asymptote, a right line that a branch of a curve is ever approaching, but never reaching. Progressive evolution is asymptotic. It will ever be approaching progress as an ideal, but never attaining it.

• • • • • •

Judson Herrick
Neurological Foundations of Animal Behavior (1924)

[I]n man the reversal of entropy reaches its highest expression in intelligent behavior...[T]he measure of human control over nature (including his own self-control) may be expressed very largely in terms of his ability to reverse entropy and to determine the patterns in which the energy thus made available shall be expended. This is creative intelligence.

. . . . . .

Since this note was written, [Frank C.] Eve (1923) has published a fascinating and stimulating survey of this field which points the way to a genuine understanding of the origins of the vital energies. He introduces two useful new terms. By *katergy* he means "the flow of energy to a lower potential or level," that is, entropy. By *anergy* he means "the flow of energy to a higher potential," that is, reversal of entropy...[I]n mankind...[the] final katergic process...is adapted to step up lower energies to the plane of intelligent adjustment, setting them to work to invent and run machines, to maintain commerce and all of the other varied industries necessary to advance personal and social welfare...This progressive increase in anergic efficiency is "creative evolution," which in our time shows no sign of abatement.

. . . . . .

Certain is it that in civilized communities the social factors have so overshadowed the individual factors that it may safely be said that further evolutionary advance will be measured by social efficiency rather than by personal efficiency alone. But the highest social efficiency is impossible without a high average of personal efficiency. What, then, is the integrating bond in such a society?...In parental care are the rudiments of that widening of the self which has culminated in the metamorphosis of a narrow self-seeking into the altruistic ideal of the highest attainable self-culture in the interest of increased value to the community as a whole. Nothing of self-interest is sacrificed in this irradiation of the personality to include in its scope the welfare of the remotest human circle, for experience has shown that the welfare of the individual is bound up with that of the society of which he forms a part. Indeed, enlightened self-interest goes further than this and includes intelligent conservation of the natural resources of forest, soil and mineral and even scenic beauty.

And so the self to be cherished and fostered has enlarged to include the family, clan. tribe, nation and (let us hope) the community of nations. Each organic unit from the cells of which the body is composed, through the tissues, organs, bodies, and human societies of successively higher rank, up to the nations which have partitioned among themselves the habitable land of the globe, is bound to the others in reciprocal organismic relationship of such a character that the welfare of each individual is essential to that of the whole and the integrity of the whole to that of even the humblest unit.

The two factors which seem to be playing the largest part at present in progressive human evolution are: (1) the greater control over nature through intelligence, ideation, and prevision of the future course of events; and (2) the progress from high individual efficiency to the still more potent cooperative unit of society.

. . . . . .

[Man's] success in the future cycles of the evolutionary movement will depend to a large extent upon the balance which he strikes between the narrower interests of his purely personal, family or national welfare and the wider relationships with his entire social environment through commerce, interchange of intellectual, esthetic and moral ideas, and sympathetic intercourse of all sorts...If we would forecast the future of progressive evolution on this planet, the question is not whether the individual human mind of to-day has greater intellectual capacity than had those of the ages of antiquity. For this we have no proper standard of measurement in any event. But the question is irrelevant. What we want to know is, does the culture of to-day exhibit better team-work than of old, is the machinery of cooperative effort more efficient, are we more neighborly, and have we a proper understanding of the searching question, who is my neighbor?

• • • • • •

George Sarton
"The New Humanism" (1924)

[H]istorical learning and teaching has dealt thus far largely with the most obvious and noisy part of human evolution, but the least important. In spite of many appearances to the contrary, man's essential purpose is not a struggle for existence or for supremacy, not a devastating scramble for the material goods of this world, but a generous and fruitful emulation in the creation and the diffusion of spiritual values. Now this creation takes place to a large extent secretly, for it is not accomplished by crowds, nor by pompous dignitaries officiating in the eyes of the people, but by individuals often poor and unknown, who carry on their sacred task in mean garrets, in wretched laboratories, or in other obscure corners scattered all over the civilized world, without hardly any regard for political boundaries, social or religious distinctions. "The wind bloweth where it listeth."

The secrecy of their work is enhanced by the fact that it goes on in spite of the catastrophies, wars and revolutions which retain the whole attention of the people...*The essential history of mankind is largely secret*. Visible history is nothing but the local scenery, the everchanging and capricious background of this invisible history which, alone, is truly œcumenical and progressive.

. . . . . .

I must especially insist upon the collaboration of East and West, because it is but too often overlooked or misunderstood. Most historians are so dominated by occidental prejudices that they can hardly imagine any other civilization than the one resulting from the double stream of Greco-Roman and Judaeo-Christian traditions; at any rate they behave as if no other civilization were worth considering...One must needs recognize that human civilization is not exclusively occidental, not by any means. Moreover the very fact that the civilizations which developed in the Mediterranean basin and in Central and Eastern Asia were largely independent, renders their comparison extremely instructive. This comparison affords another proof of the essential unity of mankind, for the fundamental problems of East and West are the same, and the solutions, however dissimilar, have yet many points of contact...[A]n immense cultural progress would be brought to pass if it were possible to combine the highest ideals of East and West. We have as much to learn from them as they from us, but we will never learn anything unless we approach one another with open hearts, and true humility.

. . . . . .

The New Humanism is a compromise between idealism and knowledge. I do not know which is worse, idealism without knowledge or knowledge without idealism, yet in the present circumstances we are but too often obliged to choose between the two evils. We need ideals to guide our steps toward the future, but they cannot possibly be fulfilled if we are not aware of the obstacles to overcome, of the paths to be followed, of the dangers that lie in them.

. . . . . .

Whatever salvation there be, is forwards not backwards. The past, however beautiful, is less beautiful than the future...The New Humanism derives its main inspiration from the past, yet it is turned towards the future.

• • • • • •

John Elof Boodin
Cosmic Evolution (1925)

The relation of individuals in society is not that of
arithmetic addition but a creative relation. This involves not
merely the creation of a new pattern, but the creation of
new units, with new characters. The whole-pattern and the
units must evolve together. Else the pattern would be
useless. The individuals must, on the one hand, have the
capacity for language and creative imagination in order to
constitute society; and, on the other hand, it is in the social
milieu that these capacities must be creatively realized.

. . . . . .

The most urgent need of creativeness to-day lies not in the
discovery of new mechanical instruments, but in the
discovery of new patterns of social co-operation, more
adapted to the needs of human nature and therefore truer
to creative nature. Our advance along the lines of
mechanical invention has outstripped our moral advance
and threatens the welfare of humanity if not its existence. It
is not likely that humanity can be destroyed by its newly
discovered murderous weapons, but it is possible that
civilization may be destroyed. It is dangerous to let a child
play with dynamite. And morally man has not passed
much beyond the savage. Man must discover a moral
formula of co-operation as broad as humanity. He must
evolve a control of mutual respect and mutual aid based
upon human beings as human beings. The mechanical
means of communication have brought human beings close

together in space, but the pattern for adaptive living together on a large scale is yet wanting, or at best is in the trial and error stage, with enormous cost to those concerned. Perhaps under the tension of stress and suffering, man may discover gradually a better way, a new equilibrium of life. Demagogues talk about public opinion and public will, but their appeal is to prejudice and their work is to create prejudice. An intelligent public opinion and public will is yet to be created, if it can be. Only when they are created, when philosophers are kings, shall we have sane government.

. . . . . .

Humanity is still impatiently prepared by heredity and still less prepared by organization for earth-wide co-operation in purposive endeavour. Perhaps the next ice-age which science prophesies may furnish the critical test of man's capacity for sympathetic co-operation.

• • • • • •

Warwick Freeman Kelloway
The Ethics of Achievement (1925)

Evolution is over the whole progressive. The various stages are physical, chemical, sensual, instinctive, conscious, creative. There is retrogression at times as well as progression. But it is over the whole progressive...The progress now lies in the field of humanity and personality, the physical development diminishing, Progress now becomes much swifter. This is seen in the advancement within the last six thousand years and especially since the Greeks. The world has entered into the social era which includes both the common good and the individual.

[T.H.] Green does not see the creative principle in nature, and [Henri] Bergson does not find the spiritual principle. If we are permitted to make a synthesis the result will be a conscious, personal, free, creative Being, going about a big work as I attempt an infinitely smaller one, not for the sake of achieving but for a purpose; not merely creative, but creating for some far-off perfection; and the process of the world becomes not an evolution nor yet a creative evolution, but a consciously creative evolution, and not merely that but the progress is a purposeful accomplishment. But are we justified in this assumption? What proof have we that it is anything more than an assumption? None. We have none whatever in mere speculation. It is only when I cease to be a spectator and enter into the work of the universe as co-creator that I have the ghost of a proof.

• • • • • •

Charles A. Ellwood
The Psychology of Human Society (1925)

While the danger in our civilization at the present time seems to be mainly from extreme individualism, yet it is evident that the other extreme, a collectivism which would suppress individual initiative and emphasize only the conformity of the individual to the group, is a possible danger which threatens the future…A balanced civilization must aim at both stability and progress in our social life, and hence leave room for individual variation, while at the same time developing through education a high type of socialized character in individuals.

. . . . . .

With the development of a tradition of progress along many cultural lines new and higher social adjustments become possible. Thus a dynamic type of civilization emerges, and slowly a tradition of progress in every line of culture is built up. Such free, reflective interference on the part of man with social conditions, institutions, and civilization does not necessarily tend to destroy social stability and order. On the contrary, even in the most progressive civilization, social habits are not apt to be discarded as long as they work well...Dynamic civilization is more durable than static civilization, because it makes possible the establishment of an equilibrium between the social life and changing conditions. In a progressive civilization, as soon as conditions change, whether in the objective environment or in knowledge and beliefs, socially adaptive processes will come in to restore the equilibrium. There need be no end, therefore, to a progressive or dynamic civilization.

But it may be asked is there not a goal for development, and is not a static condition of society and civilization bound to be reached sooner or later? The answer of social science is that, while hypothetically such a static condition of society and culture may sometime be reached, it is at present far in the future. The tradition of progress, once established in science, religion, and in the arts of life opens up ever new vistas of higher and higher social adjustments. Such ideals may be only slowly realized, but when they exist as a part of the general social pattern, they are ready to be utilized as instruments of progress as soon as the social situation calls for them. Thus we can see no end to human progress, unless the end comes through some disaster, as the result of ill-balanced development. There is, therefore, no necessary death of cultures or civilizations. If they die or even suffer serious setbacks, it is because mistakes in social adjustments were made. Dynamic civilization, if well balanced, is stable because it is a moving equilibrium in constant readjustment with the conditions of life.

• • • • • •

Dedication in Floyd (Ed.)
Social Progress: A Handbook of the Liberal Movement (1925)

To those who form conclusions from known facts and who wish to outlaw war, abolish poverty, unveil superstition and secure justice

• • • • • •

Jesse Lee Bennett
The American Tradition (1925)

[W]ith the passing of all arbitrary societies it has been hoped that there will never again be the necessity for the use of violence in giving to the laws, the "abstractions" of new order—formed inevitably by changing conditions within the shell of free institutions based on an earlier expression of abstractions—the conscious and deliberate being which the process of civilisation inexorably requires.

The process should be constant, steady, continuous, peaceful like the metabolic processes within any living organism. Change should never, henceforth, have to be sudden, violent, mechanical. It should be slow, continuous, organic.

Arbitrary societies had, perforce, a mechanical quality. They necessarily developed ideas of divine right, they required uncritical confidence and unreasoning loyalty, they prohibited *lèse majesté*. It was essential for their permanency that they be kept as static as possible and that change within them could come only by sudden, violent, and passionate catastrophes.

It is the essential necessity confronting free societies that they must, like living things, change continuously; adapt themselves continuously to the needs of the people comprising them, foster and aid the articulation of new abstractions or the rephrasing of old abstractions to render ever more satisfactorily conscious the relationships of their people.

Their political institutions being consciously based on the conscious expression of ideas entirely freed from all mystic coloring; their institutions being obvious and deliberate attempts to seek the good of the people, no idea of divine right, no uncritical allegiance and unreasoning loyalty, no *lèse majesté* is permanently possible within them. Above all, the dead hand of the past, the rigidity of organs adapted to past conditions must never be permitted to retard their wholesome evolution and development.

• • • • • •

Radhakamal Mukerjee
"Borderlands of Economics" (1925)

When economics is fully permeated with the consciousness of human value, the cleft between the mechanical and the ideal will be healed.

. . . . . .

The acquisitive and possessive impulses which have been so much exaggerated in the last few decades will, we believe, in the next few decades be duly limited in vital modes of association, and the separation between intrinsic or final and instrumental or economic ends which has threatened to corrode social life will no longer warp the feeling and judgment of people. Final or ideal values will be imported into the common daily life of toiling humanity and will lend it a grace and dignity born of the consciousness of its place in a vast scheme of things. Economic activity will be both a means of social service, and an opportunity for personal self-realisation; it will become a sort of daily sacrament. Economic thought and planning will be inspired by the genius of the race which will declare to the individual its evolutionary purpose even as it has planned for bees and ants the polity of the hive or nest, and for every region or group Nature and Man will envisage a distinctive pattern, making manifest in time its portion of eternal beauty and wisdom. The different economic ends will attain a unity of character as the creation of one myriad-minded Economist who is speaking through the ages in the accents of history for the cessation of the eternal disparity between might and right, between property and poverty, between enjoyment and creation.

The economy of the earth will thus be transfigured and the economics of peoples related to the economics of humanity.

• • • • • •

Carrie Chapman Catt
"Evolution—Fifty Years Ago" (1925)

I left...college grounded in the faith that Evolution would allow no permanent harm to come to the race through its stupidity and blunders; that Evolution would move faster and avoid pitfalls if there were plenty of sensible "evolutors" who would try to think straight, and act accordingly. I make no claim to achievement but I have spent my life in a sincere endeavor to help God's law of Evolution evolve.

• • • • • •

Alfred North Whitehead
Science and the Modern World (1925)

The world is now faced with a self-evolving system, which it cannot stop. There are dangers and advantages in this situation. It is obvious that the gain in material power affords opportunity for social betterment. If mankind can rise to the occasion, there lies in front a golden age of beneficent creativeness.

• • • • • •

J.M. Beck

Comments about Edward Dean Adams upon Adams'
award of the John Fritz Medal (1926)

If there be one enigma which thoughtful men of all nations
are now considering more deeply than at any previous time
in history, it is whether the high potential of dynamic
power either raises or lowers the high potential of man's
spiritual nature. In other words, whether the excessive
mechanization of human life is not leading to certain evils
that may well give concern to all who try, timidly at best, to
scan the future.

It would be easy to demonstrate the enormous part that
mechanical invention had played in the progress of
mankind. But on the other hand, there are many wise and
thoughtful men who perceive that an excessive
mechanization of human society is bound to have baleful
and portentous effects upon the human spirit. It is the
greatest problem with which, in my judgment, humanity
has to deal.

If there be any solution of this question, it lies, it seems
to me, in a class of men, true leaders in human life, being
developed, who are men of telescopic, rather than of
microscopic brain.

With the mechanization of human society, human
society becomes complex; and as it becomes complex, there
is an unavoidable tendency to specialize; and as men
become more specialized, of necessity there is a certain
disintegration and a lack of solidarity of the social forces of
human life. One remedy for that is to develop a class of
leadership in the community of men of telescopic brains,
who are not merely the devotees of any one branch of
human activity, but whose minds are broad and have a

natural taste and interest for everything that pertains to mankind.

• • • • • •

Ellsworth Faris

"The Nature of Human Nature" (1926)

Despite the chauvinists, the cynics, and the absolutists of every sort, human nature can be changed. Indeed, if one speaks with rigorous exactness, human nature never ceases to be altered; for the crises in life and nature, the interaction and diffusion of exotic cultures, and the varying temperaments possessed by the troops of continuously appearing and gradually begotten children force the conclusion that human nature is in a continual state of flux. We cannot change it by passing a law, nor by a magical act of the will, nor by ordering and forbidding, nor by day-dreaming and revery, but human nature can be changed. To defend militarism on the ground that man is a fighter and the fighting instinct cannot be changed is merely to misinterpret and to rationalize an important fact: that the custom of warfare is very old and can be abolished only gradually and with great difficulty. To assume that the drinking habits of a people or their economic structure or even the family organization is immutably founded upon the fixed patterns of human nature is to confuse nature and custom. What we call the stable elements of human nature are in truth the social attitudes of individual persons, which in turn are the subjective aspects of long-established group attitudes whose inertia must be reckoned with but whose mutability cannot be denied. Having been established through a long period of time, and appearing to the youth as normal and natural, they seem to be part of the ordered universe. In reality they are continually being slightly altered and may at any time be profoundly modified by a sufficiently serious crisis in the life of the group.

The history of social movements is but a record of changing human nature. The antislavery movement, the woman's movement, the temperance movement, the interestingly differing youth movements in Germany, China, and America—these are all natural phenomena in the field of sociology, and are perhaps most accurately described as the process of change which human nature undergoes in response to the pressure of unwelcome events giving rise to restlessness and vague discontent. Such movements, when they generate leaders and develop institutions passing on to legal and political changes, create profound alterations of the mores and thoroughly transform not only the habits of a people and their nature as they live together but also the basic conception of what constitutes human nature. The present conception in the West of the nature of woman, including her mental capacity and ability to do independent creative work, is profoundly different from the conception which anybody entertained in the generations before the woman's movement began.

• • • • • •

William H. Kilpatrick
Education for a Changing Civilization (1926)

That social change promises...to increase so rapidly is in itself possibly the most momentous change in historic times. Up to recently the rate of change has been so slow that philosophy and morals could in essential degree affect

240

to ignore change. That time seems, however, now to have passed. Change has become too obvious, too inclusive. Our young people face too clearly an unknown future. We dare not pretend that the old solutions will suffice for them. It appears that we must have a philosophy that not only takes positive recognition of the fact of change but one that includes within it change as an essential element.

. . . . . .

Various writers have made us familiar with the conception of social lag. Progress is seldom uniform. Strain comes from the uneven front thus kept. For us here perhaps the most interesting instance of this is where through mechanical inventions new ways of living are introduced and the regulative social-moral outlook and ways of behaving lag behind. Thus at the present time industrialism has greatly changed American living, but our general legal and moral outlooks remain much the same as when life was largely rural and agricultural. If mechanical inventions come with ever increasing frequency and our ways of living change accordingly, surely our moral outlook must keep abreast of other changes or society may suffer greatly.

...What is to be done? A figure from another field may suggest the line of attack. A spinning top not only stands upright but even resists efforts to push it over. When its motion stops, it falls. Movement itself may bring stability. In the bicycle we see an even clearer analogy to our situation. To keep it upright, we must make it run along. May there not be found an analogous "moving equilibrium" for our social affairs? Laying aside the figure, we may distinguish in the present social situation three stages of change. First, are such changes in effecting ordinary material ends as better lighting, better means of transportation, better disposal of sewage. These in turn bring about, second, such changes as the modern city with its enormous population living largely in apartment houses –conditions that in one way or another bring apparently bad effects on family life. The third change we have not so far made, namely, the satisfactory adjustment of family life to the new conditions surrounding it.

As we consider these three stages of change, most people in this country have hithero counted it either not feasible or not desirable to hinder either the first or the second kind. Inventions and their use have on the whole been accepted and encouraged. There are, to be sure, those who attempt to resist them, but their influence is usually quite limited and in large measure death ends the effort at opposition. But it is not so with the third kind of change. When it comes to changing the hithero customary moral-social outlook, no matter how inadequate it may have become, opposition here proves powerful. A senseless inertia seems, too, about as effective as conscious opposition. One sad feature is that conscience easily allies itself with the lagging outlook. Well intentioned men direct great moral energy in such way as to increase the lag. If there be such a thing as moving social equilibrium, dynamic social stability, it should belong right here and would seem to consist in the disposition and ability to keep the moral-social vision and grasp abreast of the social changes otherwise introduced. To help bring about and maintain such a dynamic equilibrium, to help develop the necessary moral vision and grasp—this, of course, is the great duty of the efficient educational system.

. . . . . .

[W]hat outcomes are we to seek?...On the one hand, our young people must build such dynamic outlook, insight, habits, and attitudes as will enable them to hold their course amid change. To do this, they must, as they grow older, increase in the ability to stand on their own feet—to decide matters wisely for themselves. We, their elders, must in the end renounce and all claim to sovereignty over them. No longer can one generation bind the next to its solutions. On the other hand, our young people must learn such general and flexible techniques as promise best to serve them in that unknown future. We cannot know their precise problems, still less the answers to their problems. But we can in some measure forecast the general run and outline of their problems. We can give them effective access to our stock of useful data. We can in particular give them an intelligent control over the best methods of attack, including the method of criticizing methods. All this in order that the rising generation may be as effectively prepared as we can help it to be for that unknown and shifting future which confronts.

• • • • • •

Edmund Noble
Purposive Evolution (1926)

The world fashions itself anew for us, and all the more grandly, as we realize that the objects we have so long intellectually separated form a together, an interdependent, interdetermining totality, every unit and area of it system-sourced—that as human intelligence derived from cosmic intelligence we are really one with the universe we contemplate, strong with its power and sharing in its work, however subject to its process. As our midnight constellations grew not less but more beautiful to the race because it ceased to think of them as deified animals and men, so our woods take on a new glory when, instead of viewing plant, insect and bird as products of consciously imposed plan, we recognize in them the intelligence, the freedom and the wonder of delegated universe power. To be convinced that the process which reveals itself within us as purpose is the same process that spreads the spider's web, builds up the flower, shapes the crystal, presides over the gathering of the planets and guides the marshaling of suns, is to make Nature dear to us beyond the lure of myth or the persuading of poetry. And with Nature thus refashioned, man undergoes a like transfiguration. Behind each act of helpfulness to one's fellows, to one's group, to one's kind stretch the countless acts which make up the sum of human experience. Related to all doings in the past, to all doings in the present, to all doings in the future, conduct comes up and in to us charged with deep and solemn meanings. The soul of things unseen enters into the simplest service we give or receive; the labor for which we pay or are paid grows rich beyond all thought of its money value; for the broader vision, all days seem sacred which the sun bestows on its planetary family, and each hour given to worthy effort is consecrated.

Only as we persist in reading human motives and meanings into the cosmos will Nature, life and man continue to demand justifications which they do not need, and to arouse expectations which they cannot satisfy. Pessimism, like the "problem of evil," is for the subjective view alone. If differences are required for knowledge, action must also have its contrasts if we are to have any sense of values. If there is to be advance from bad to good, and from good to better, the world must be a process, as well as an extension, and there must be struggle as well as change: better the busy strife of an ant-hill, with life growing from more to more, than a whole universe made perfect at the cost of stagnation. Errors to be dispelled, wrongs to be overcome, faulty individual adjustments to be set right, social and political adjustments to be improved — these are our opportunities in a régime where the what is, however determined by past and present, is being continually transformed by the what ought to be.

• • • • • •

E.A. Burroughs, Bishop of Ripon
Address to members of the British Association for the
Advancement of Science (1927)

With all his new mastery over nature, man has not seemed really to be advancing his own cause. The development of his resources has not helped either development or happiness for himself. Until this disproportion is somehow rectified man cannot feel safe, and the very greatness of his recent achievements would seem to make his ruin more certain and more complete.

We could get on very much more happily if aviation, wireless, television and the like were advanced no further than at present.

Dare I even suggest, at the risk of being lynched by some of my hearers, that the sum of human happiness, outside of scientific circles would not necessarily be reduced if for, say ten years, every physical and chemical laboratory were closed and the patient and resourceful energy displayed in them transferred to recovering the lost art of getting together and finding a formula for making the ends meet in the scale of human life?

It would give 99 per cent of us who are non-scientific some chance of assimilating the revolutionary knowledge which in the first quarter of this century 1 per cent of the explorers have acquired. The 1 per cent, who would have leisure to read up on one another's work; and all of us might go meanwhile in tardy quest of that wisdom which is other than and greater than knowledge and without which knowledge may be a curse.

As things stand today, we could get on without further additions for the present to our knowledge of nature. We cannot get on without a change of mind in man.

● ● ● ● ● ●

Charles Ellwood
Cultural Evolution (1927)

Culture is necessarily a product of cooperation...The struggle of man for food, against the adverse forces of nature, against disease, against crime, will probably tax the resources of human cooperation in the future to the utmost. Therefore man must learn to transcend war if he is to continue to advance in culture. If enlightenment can be spread through universal education, war, like slavery, should prove to be but a transitional process between the lower and more primitive phases of culture and the higher phases yet to be realized. Moreover, if we can unlearn the war process and devote ourselves to the productive and constructive phases of culture, it would seem probable that all of the unsocial and irrational ideas and ideals which have been associated with war and its typical cultural products would in time disappear. This is of course a mere hypothesis, but it is at least reasonable and based upon a study of the visible trend of culture.

. . . . . .

If the learning process in human society can go on uninterruptedly, there should be no swing-backs in culture. We should have only those plateaus which we find also in the learning of the individual...There is real analogy, or rather identity, between the learning process in an individual and in a social group. The process is simply more complex in the latter case because of the great number of individuals involved. In both cases, it is essentially a modification and accumulation of habit complexes. But just as there are chances for the individual to start wrong habits which interfere with the further normal development of the learning process, so there are many more chances of a human group's starting habits or institutions which will interfere with the normal development of its culture, or even bring about a reversion in culture. There are many such habits and institutions. Most of them seem merely to produce a static condition in culture; but others, like war and luxury, so interrupt the learning process that they produce actual reversions in culture.

The fact that cultures start anew after such a reversion is due to the fact that man is inevitably a learner, and that he learns even from his mistakes and calamities. The freeing of the process of learning in the group gives rise, accordingly, to a new start or a new lead in culture.

. . . . . .

Whether we believe that the scientific method and the diffusion of the scientific attitude can...safeguard our civilization or not, it is at least important to see that there is no inevitable law of decline or decadence in the cultural process, but that, on the contrary, all cultural decadence is due to the interruption of the collective learning process. This, in turn, may be traced to the blunders, mistakes, and errors in judgment of leaders and of the masses. The development of science, especially of social science, should work to prevent this, especially if the cooperation of the masses of mankind with scientific leaders can be secured. Reversions in culture are, it would seem, no more inevitable than famine, pestilence, or war. All these, to be sure, have characterized the history of mankind; but science believes that they can all be eliminated and prevented.

What sort of social and cultural evolution can we look forward to under the guidance of science? To answer this, let us recall that the evolution which man is undergoing is not primarily a physical nor even a mental evolution; *it is primarily a cultural evolution*...Man's mental evolution manifestly depends upon the advance in culture. Man does not increase his intellectual capacities, but he accumulates, rationalizes, and diffuses his knowledge. General enlightenment is not due to individual advance, but to cultural advance...The whole evolution of man from the beginning of his existence upon this planet to the end is necessarily an evolution which is dominantly cultural and which will be increasingly dominated by culture.

If now we look ahead rather than backward, we shall be able to project the trend of human evolution. With this spread of enlightenment through universal education, there will be more and more acceptance of the scientific spirit and method in all phases of culture. Even in its non-material phases, the aberrations and crude experiments of the past will tend to straighten out. Gradually the advance of culture will become more smooth and even; but completer adjustments will also be attained and the upward trend of culture in all its phases will be less noticeable. Civilization will no longer be a crude process of trial and error, and no longer illy balanced, but will move forward steadily to greater harmony and consistency between all of its parts. In a word, culture will be socialized, rationalized, and beautified. Full civilization, in distinction from the partial civilization which the past has enjoyed, will arise.

Let us now try again to construct the total curve of the evolution of man, beginning as man leaves the animal world at the point of his creation, and continuing until he passes again from this planet into the darkness of oblivion. The curve of his evolution, as we have said, is the curve of the development of his culture from animality to humanity, from brutality to spirituality. The whole development of culture will then present itself as a parabola with the aberrations most intense as it passes around its focus. The complexity of the stream of culture may defy scientific analysis; but the direction of the stream is clear. It moves, though slowly and not without interruptions, toward the development of the distinctly human; namely of the rational, the social, and the esthetic elements in man's life. Even if this curve is only a play of fancy, it serves at least to indicate to us where we are in the process of human evolution and why things are as they are in our world at the present moment (see Figure 17).

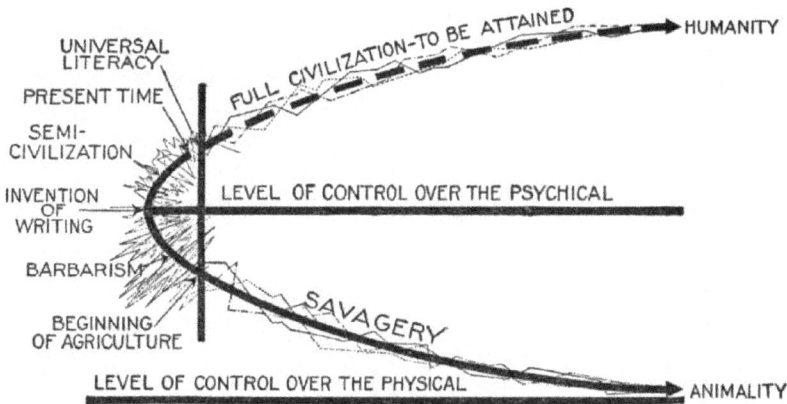

FIGURE 17
The Stream of Civilization. (The finer lines symbolize the various cultural traditions.)

• • • • • •

J.O. Hertzler
"Social Immortality" (1928)

[H]umanity is an ever-growing and perfecting whole with which the active individual merges and thus through his works becomes a factor in the eternal human and social process…In essence [this] concept conceives of humanity as a continuous whole, including the past, the present, and the future; a progressive realization through time of the intellectual and moral and spiritual potentialities contained in human nature; the sum-total of all dead, living, or future beings who have voluntarily labored for the progress and blessedness of man.

…The validity of this concept rests upon the fact of the perpetuity of ideas, ideals, and acts—in brief, of achievement. What you do in your life work determines one sort of immortality you are going to have. It is the immortality of influence-values. It is an extension into the future of personal and social values created by the individual...According to this doctrine the inconceivable millions of humble strivers that have preceded us, the obscure and simple creatures that have undauntedly been living the best life that they knew, are recognized as having their part in the on-flowing good life...It also includes the positive contributions of the great body of achievers, both influential and unknown, of the present, and the incalculable additions of the men of future ages; each in his separate place adding to the sum total of human and social good.

...[This doctrine] presents mankind as a single, interconnected, interrelated, and continuous whole...It rests securely on the great evolutionary fact of universal continuity, which is true, whether we will or not, in the social world, as in the physical, biological, or chemical. As the individual grasps this fact he sees himself reaping where others have sown; and he sows in his turn with confidence that the germinal process of civilization will bring his efforts to fruition in the ages to come.

......

A realization of the fact of cumulative social good such as the one here discussed, evokes an emotional fervor which tends to enlist the whole intelligence and activity and enthusiasm of the thinking man in the creation of social and human values and the performance of socially profitable and progressive acts...He sees himself as the present container of the stream of life—a stream which has had an unbroken flow on this earth through millions of years.

......

It is said that the flight of a sparrow affects the equilibrium of the universe. So also the efforts of the man of humble calling are not without their influence. But as there is no instrument as yet delicate enough to register the effects of the sparrow's flight, so the works of the humble man do not loom up in a spectacular way like those of the great men. Certainly, though, every act of every individual, good or bad, has its influences and leaves its impress on the future. The work of every individual, though it may pass without notice, can never be wasted. It enters into the life of the community, and continues, ever developing, to the end of time.

. . . . . .

[T]here is no more accurate measure of a man's civilization than the distance into the future to which he projects his efforts and his satisfactions. Some men must have their satisfactions within twenty-four hours, or there is no stimulus to effort; others in ten years; others during their lifetime; others must be assured of it for their children; while some will, without a thought of self, see all the way, and live for posterity. They are the men who build in the present the foundations for the fulfillment of man's best aspirations. It seems more than possible that the extent and scope of a man's aspirations are the measure of his immortality.

• • • • • •

Robert A. Millikan
"Science and Modern Life" (1928)

Within the past half century, as a direct result of the findings of modern science, there has developed an evolutionary philosophy — an evolutionary religion, too, if you will — which has given a new emotional basis to life, the most inspiring and the most forward-looking that the world has thus far seen.

. . . . . .

> A fire-mist and a planet,
> A crystal and a cell,
> A jellyfish and a saurian,
> And caves where the cavemen dwell;
> Then a sense of law and beauty,
> And a face turned from the clod —
> Some call it Evolution,
> And others call it God.

That sort of sentiment is the gift of modern science to the world. And there is one further finding of modern science which has a tremendous inspirational appeal. It is the discovery of the vital part which we ourselves are playing in this evolutionary process. For man himself has within two hundred years discovered new forces with the aid of which he is now consciously and very rapidly making over both his physical and his biological environment. The Volta Centenary, a symbol of our electrical age, was representative of the one, the stamping out of yellow fever is an illustration of the other. And if the biologist is right that the biological evolution of the human organism is going on so slowly that man himself is not now endowed with capacities appreciably different from those which he brought with him into the period of recorded history, then since, within this period, the forward strides that he has made in his control over his environment, in the development of his civilization, have been stupendous and unquestionable, it follows that this progress has been due, not to the betterment of his stock, but rather primarily to the passing on of the accumulated knowledge of the race to the generations following after. The great instruments of progress for mankind are then research — the discovery of new knowledge — and education — the passing on of the store of accumulated wisdom to our followers. This puts the immediate destinies of the race or of our section of the race, or of our section of our country, largely in our own hands.

. . . . . .

[O]ur modern world is distinctive not for the discovery of new modes of expression or new fields of knowledge, though it has opened up enough of these, but for the discovery of the very idea of progress, for the discovery of the method by which progress comes about, and for inspiring the world with confidence in the values of that method. So long as the world can be kept thus inspired, it is difficult to see how a relapse to another dark age can take place.

Even if the biological evolution of the human race should not continue, — though why should what has been going on for millions of years have come to an end just now? — yet the process by which progress has been made within historic times can scarcely fail to be continuously operative. This process is the discovery of new knowledge by each generation and the transmission to the following generation of the accumulated accomplishment of the past — the discovery of new truth and the passing on of old truth.

The importance of both elements in this process has not been realized in the past, and dark ages have come. But the means for the spread of knowledge, for its preservation and transmission, the facilities for universal education and inspiration, the time for leisure, and the opportunity for thought for everybody — all these have been so extended by modem science, and are capable of such further extension, that no prophecy of decline can possibly have any scientific foundation Even arguing solely by the method of extrapolation from the past, modern science has shown that the ups and downs on the curve of history are superposed upon a curve whose general trend is upward, and it has therefore brought forth a certain amount of justification for the faith that it will continue to be upward. In the last analysis, humanity has but one supreme problem, the problem of kindling the torch of enlightened creative effort, here and there and everywhere, and of passing on for the enrichment of the lives of future generations the truth already discovered — in two words, the problem of research and of education.

●　●　●　●　●　●

H.G. Wells

The Open Conspiracy (1928/1933)

The world is undergoing immense changes. Never before have the conditions of life changed so swiftly and enormously as they have changed for mankind in the last fifty years. We have been carried along—with no means of measuring the increasing swiftness in the succession of events. We are only now beginning to realize the force and strength of the storm of change that has come upon us.

These changes have not come upon our world from without. No meteorite from outer space has struck our planet; there have been no overwhelming outbreaks of volcanic violence or strange epidemic diseases; the sun has not flared up to excessive heat or suddenly shrunken to plunge us into Arctic winter. The changes have come through men themselves. Quite a small number of people, heedless of the ultimate consequence of what they did, one man here and a group there, have made discoveries and produced and adopted inventions that have changed all the condition, of social life.

We are now just beginning to realize the nature of these changes, to find words and phrases for them and put them down. First they began to happen, and then we began to see that they were happening. And now we are beginning to see how these changes are connected together and to get the measure of their consequences. We are getting our minds so clear about them that soon we shall be able to demonstrate them and explain them to our children in our schools. We do not do so at present. We do not give our children a chance of discovering that they live in a world of universal change...

It was only in the beginning of the twentieth century that people began to realize the real significance of that aspect of our changing conditions to which the phrase "the abolition of distance" has been applied. For a whole century before that there had been a continual increase in the speed and safety of travel and transport and the ease and swiftness with which messages could be transmitted, but this increase had not seemed to be a matter of primary importance. Various results of railway, steamship, and telegraph became manifest; towns grew larger, spreading into the countryside, once inaccessible lands became areas of rapid settlement and cultivation, industrial centres began to live on imported food, news from remote parts lost its time-lag and tended to become contemporary, but no one hailed these things as being more than "improvements" in existing conditions. They are not observed to be the beginnings of a profound revolution in the life of mankind.

• • • • • •

Radhakamal Mukerjee
"The Ecological Outlook in Sociology" (1932)

A society undergoing rapid change is...characterized by rapid changes of occupation, of economic and social status, and of location of individuals and change of social standards and ideals. The movement of population, a change in methods of production and in distribution of wealth, or new standards and ideals of living, which precede a new social gradation, all indicate a transformation of the ecological base and consequent transformation of the dynamic relations between the different parts of the life-community.

The cultural order is woven within the skeleton of the ecological order, and it is the intermeshing of the two orders, organic and spiritual, which sets before us the complex web of the whole life-community in its completeness. As evolution progresses, the organization of life and mind in the region shows greater correlation and solidarity, on the one hand, and extension and continuity on the other...A permanent form of agricultural and sylvicultural activity can furnish the only basis of a permanent civilization, and this implies the conservation of the region, and of its intricate and fateful ecologic forces, which is far removed from the present lack of occupational balance, and manifold economic and social wastes. Economic equilibrium can be attained only if people and occupations in different levels of the valley section work harmoniously together for the uplift of the entire region.

. . . . . .

Co-operation, scientific and broad-minded, with the ecologic forces which have stamped the region with a unity and individuality ought to be the keynote of the future. The conservation of soil, water and food, the economy of man's food and energy circulation, the protection of the earth's mantle of trees and grasses, the selection and crossing of crops, trees and animals, the biological control or eradication of diseases, pests and parasites, the utilization of all kinds of organic wastage, permanent agriculture, the conservation of water supply and the training and management of rivers and water courses, a nicely adjusted occupational balance which may best utilize the resources and possibilities of different sections of the region and the skill and aptitudes of the people—all this is social ecology. Through the ages, as he has increased his numbers and his dominance, man has committed crime against sun and water, plants and animals, robbed in record time organisms and habitats that have been economically beneficial, introduced his own appurtenances in the way of domesticated animals and cultivated plants, and disfigured the ground with the traces of his labors and devices, too often letting loose destructive forces which have impoverished and ultimately engulfed his civilization even in the most favored regions. Nature's processes of change are slow but sure. Man's quick methods of adjustment have often proved harmful in the long run, and enormous wastage of human toil and skill has followed in the wake of his startlingly quick achievements. Man must to some extent imitate Nature's extraordinarily slow methods. In Nature the communities of life consisting of many different species found in a region are slow growths, but these are balanced and interlaced growths, selection being largely determined by the established system of linkages and correlations of organisms. The more surely does man adjust his own life to the processes and communities of life of his region, the more will he elicit Nature's enormous reserves of capital and energy for maintaining the continuity of himself and of his works, experiences and institutions in the region. Man's future advance lies, indeed, in a bio-economic co-operation, based on the scientific comprehension of the complex web of life that comprises both the living and the non-living realms, and this is deeper than, and goes beyond, co-operation merely within the human community.

. . . . . .

[M]ere scientific understanding of the web of life does not help matters. Man should cultivate a new humility and a new foresight in the interest of unborn societies of the future, which will be religious in its significance, before he can make himself the enduring and central link in the vital chain of food and energy circulation on the earth of which his pattern of civilization is but a phase, and so far a passing one.

Briefly speaking, the influence of the region on the whole life-community and of the life-community on the region expresses the maintenance of specific normal pattern and activity. In ecology, plant, animal or human, we never get away from the specific pattern of life. The conception of a specific normal pattern of life and its maintenance is here fundamental, whether we are considering the inter-relations of great harmonic vegetable or animal aggregations which have arrived at a more or less stable equilibrium in the region, or the inter-linkages of economic, social or political arrangements. The pattern of life is an actively maintained whole, at first confined to but later transcending the boundaries of time and space, and both the structure and life-activities of its component communities, subhuman and human, are manifestations of this organic unity.

The presence or absence of a single factor thus changes the whole pattern of life from non-living to living and cultural levels...The pattern of life, fashioned first by the physical and chemical characters of the environment, shows a specific co-ordinated unity of structure and activity also in its radiations and extensions in the spheres of culture and tradition. It grows and evolves as a whole, bringing about a harmony of the lesser and simpler with the greater and more complex wholes of Nature. In the subtle ways of Nature, sun and earth, plants and animals mingle silently with mind, society and culture and become part of their structure. The region and the life-community in their reciprocal give-and-take thus record the gradual development and stratification of progressive series of wholes, stretching from the inorganic beginnings to the highest levels of spiritual creation. We thus reach by another line of reasoning Smut's conception of Holism.

The creative intensified Field of Nature, consisting of all physical organic and personal wholes in their close interactions and mutual influences, is itself of an organic or holistic character—that Field is the source of the grand Ecology of the Universe. It is the environment, the Society—vital, friendly, educative, creature of all wholes and all souls.

The trend of evolution, which ecology envisages, is for the pattern of life to attain greater and greater solidarity and permanence through friendly, intimate, and subtle linkages. What is organic in Nature and shapes her ends blindly and haphazardly becomes purposive in human society, and thus the pattern of life, spiritual and teleologically progressive, crosses the boundaries of time and space. Bio-ecologic co-operation or, to use another term, symbiosis, organic and social, is the key to the permanence of man's civilization, his works and experiences on the earth. May not this be a faint glimpse of that majestic symbiosis of the Universe brought about by the harmony of the varied forces of Nature, of gravitation, light, time, the unseen rays or the sidereal influences, which has woven for man's vision through the ages the synoptic conception of Absolute Truth, Beauty, and Goodness?

• • • • • •

Joseph McCabe
Can We Save Civilisation? (1932)

It would hardly be inaccurate to say that for the first time in the long story of life on earth unconscious evolution is becoming conscious evolution; that the human race is at last deliberately choosing the lines of its development. There have, of course, been ages in which small civilisations have had a fairly complete sense of mastery of their own collective life, even though these lacked the idea of progressive evolution. But there was never before an age in which all properly educated people in all lands conceived the entire race as an organism that not only can change the character of its life, but is impelled by what it knows about its past and its future to effect such a change; to rid itself of the lingering blunders of the past and recognise the law of progress. This conception of the power and right, if not duty, of the human family to organise its life, as a whole and in every detail, in its own interest, in the light of the truth that it is passing from inferior to higher stages, ought to be made the fundamental creed of all, whatever philosophies or theosophies individuals may choose to combine with it. I express it, for brevity, in abstract terms, but it is a creed that, as I know from experience, can be taught to slum-children of twelve summers, and it holds such promise of assuaging pain and eliminating misery that it has the highest inspirational value.

• • • • • •

William F. Ogburn and Seabury C. Gilfillan
"The Influence of Invention and Discovery" (1933)

A society interested in where it is going will find it important to concern itself with the question of what types of invention should be encouraged...The wishes of society are not...the sole determinants of invention...Still, it is important to question the social valuations in regard to invention, particularly as to the relative amount of encouragement given to social invention as compared with mechanical invention.

Indeed, instead of comparing the attention given to social and mechanical invention, it might be well to ask first whether society wishes to encourage mechanical invention and natural science at all. The question appears either absurd or academic, yet the changes which many conservatives object to are the result of invention. And even radicals have suggested "declaring a moratorium" on invention until society catches up.

. . . . . .

The problem of adaptation is characterized by a time element. The inventions occur first, and only later do the institutions of society change in conformity. Material culture and social institutions are not independent of each other, for civilization is highly articulated like a piece of machinery, so that a change in one part tends to effect changes in other parts—but only after a delay. Man with habits and society with patterns of action are slow to change to meet the new material conditions...Technology seems to change sooner than do social institutions. Society will hardly decide to discourage science and invention, for these have added knowledge and have brought material welfare. And as to the difficulties and problems they create, the solution would seem to lie not so much in discouraging natural science as in encouraging social science.

The problem of the better adaptation of society to its large and changing material culture and the problem of lessening the delay in this adjustment are cardinal problems for social science. It seems very difficult to anticipate inventions and their social effects.

• • • • • •

Alfred North Whitehead
Adventures of Ideas (1933)

A race may exhaust a form of civilization without having exhausted its own creative springs of originality. In that case, a quick period of transition may set in, which may or may not be accompanied by dislocations involving widespread unhappiness. Such periods are Europe at the close of the Middle Ages, Europe during the comparatively long Reformation Period, Europe at the end of the eighteenth century. Also let us hope that our present epoch is to be viewed as a period of change to a new direction of civilization, involving in its dislocations a minimum of human misery. And yet surely the misery of the Great War was sufficient for any change of epoch.

These quick transitions to new types of civilizations are only possible when thought has run ahead of realization. The vigour of the race has then pushed forward into the adventure of imagination, so as to anticipate the physical adventures of exploration. The world dreams of things to come, and then in due season arouses itself to their realization...

Sometimes adventure is acting within limits. It can then calculate its end, and reach it. Such adventures are the ripples of change within one type of civilization, by which an epoch of given type preserves its freshness. But, given the vigour of adventure, sooner or later the leap of imagination reaches beyond the safe limits of the epoch, and beyond the safe limits of learned rules of taste. It then produces the dislocations and confusions marking the advent of new ideals for civilized effort.

A race preserves its vigour so long as it harbours a real contrast between what has been and what may be; and so long as it is nerved by the vigour to adventure beyond the safeties of the past. Without adventure civilization is in full decay.

• • • • • •

Arnold H. Kamiat
"The Basis of Society" (1934)

A serious error has crept into the thought expended on social problems...[T]he error consists in a failure to conceive a problem in terms of the greater whole of which it is a part, and to perceive that an adequate solution of the problem is unattainable without a correlated treatment of the larger problem. In fine, the complete solution of a social problem involves the transfiguration of society and of its component parts. How does the error in question manifest itself?

When it is a question of the solution of an economic problem, a remedy, couched in economic terms, is suggested. If it is a political problem that it is desired to settle, solutions in terms of political transformation are broached. For the marital question, a sociological prescription is offered. If it is the question of international relations that is the object of attention, the suggested answer will make its appeal to international law, diplomacy, ethnology, and political science. Biological problems call forth a eugenic programme, problems of crime a criminological and penological prescription. For the solution of the problems connected with law and its execution, jurisprudence is appealed to. In fine, social problems are treated as independent wholes bearing no necessary relation to each other. The problems are simply collocated, and to each problem there is equated a solution, the latter generally couched in terms of the art or science within the province of which the related problem is held to lie. All of which is justifiable, but only when it is used in connection with another and more important method.

The error that has just been mentioned consists of the utter neglect of the latter. The method in question is the conception of the unity of all social problems and of the consequent necessity of their joint solution by means of a gradual and fundamental transfiguration of society and its integral parts—individuals, societies, and institutions. Society is one. Its problems are one. No one of these problems can be adequately treated except in so far as the society and the general social disharmony of which the problem is a segment are attended to. The solution of the social problem is one.

. . . . . .

The need for a sociological monism has long ago received recognition. And in response thereto false monisms have reared their heads. Foremost among these is that which derives all problems from the economic one. The solution of all social problems is contingent upon the solution of the economic one...Then there is the biological monism...How shall a genuine sociological monism be arrived at? Perhaps this question is more easily answered after a close examination of the fallacy of the false monisms of the sort that have just been treated. The fallacy lies in this, that it is sought to explain a multiplicity of objects in terms of one class of them. Or to put it differently, it is sought to explain several categories of social phenomena in terms of one of these categories. This represents an attempt to interpret a whole in terms of a part, conceived not as a part, but a cause of the whole!

. . . . . .

The essence of society, that which makes society society, is its basis. Enough has already been said to dispose of the economic and biological monisms. Neither the economic nor the biological can be classified as basic, for neither can be said to be independent and to rest on nothing beyond itself...That which has been said concerning the economic and the biological can be asserted with reference to the political, the juridical, the cultural, the moral, the religious, and any other segment of the social order that may be classed as basic...Herein lies the basis of society: in its unity, its wholeness, its self-consistency. Society is an entity, containing parts, bearing certain relations to one another. Every part and every relation has its setting within this whole—it rests therein, has its roots therein. It has its widest social meanings determined by and within the whole.

. . . . . .

If integrity is basis, and the wider integration is fundamental with reference to included and lesser integrations, then the social order must itself rest on a larger order, and ultimately on the largest order conceivable. This is equivalent to the statement that it rests finally on the ultimate principle of order, whatsoever it might be. And it is there that the most ultimate basis of society is to be found. Further, it is in terms of this ultimate integrative principle that all problems of social construction and reconstruction are to be approached. This means an end to the business of wrenching something out of the social context, placing it beneath the social structure, and terming it a basis. It means an end to the destructively harmful fallacy that social progress must halt at all points but one, misconceived as fundamental, and mark time while progress at that point is completed. It means a conception of progress as distributed, simultaneous, carried on with a due regard for the balance and the rhythm and the order of the whole.

• • • • • •

J.L. Moreno
Who Shall Survive? (1934)

The weakest point in our present day universe is the incapacity of man to meet the machine, the cultural conserve, or the robot, otherwise than through submission, actual destruction, and social revolution. The problem of remaking man himself and not alone his environment has become the outstanding problem the more successfully technical forces prosper in the realization of the machine, the cultural conserve and the robot; and although the development of these is far from having reached its peak, the final situation of man and his survival can be clearly visualized, at least theoretically.

First, one may ask how it is possible that a machine-like device can become dangerous to man as a creator. Following the course of man throughout the various stages of our civilization, we find him using the same methods in the making of cultural products which are used later and with less friction by the products of his mind, his technical devices. These methods have always amounted simply to this—to neglect and abandon the genuine and outstanding creative process in him, to extinguish all the active, living moments, and to strive towards one unchangeable goal: the illusion of the finished, perfected product whose assumed perfectibility was an excuse par excellence for forsaking its past, for preferring one partial phenomenon to the whole reality. There is a shrewd motive in this procedure of man because if only one stage of a creative process is a really good one, and all the others are bad, then this chosen stage substituting for the entire process can be memorized, conserved, eternalized, and can give comfort to the soul of the creator and order to the civilization of which he is a part.

We can observe this strategy in all the cultural attempts of man and this strategy could deceive man and be regarded as worthy and beneficial as long as the process of industrial revolution did not produce an unprecedented world situation. As long as the mechanical device did not enter *en masse* into the economic situation in the form of the book, the gramophone, and the talking film, man had no competition in the execution of his conserves. Once an ensemble of actors had rehearsed and acquired a play to perfection, this ensemble was the only owner of their particular bit of merchandise which they offered for sale. Their only competition could come from another group of persons. Once a group of musicians had rehearsed and perfected a certain number of musical compositions, they were the only owners and executors of this product. Through the process of repetition they earned money. The introduction of cultural devices changed the situation completely. Man was not needed any more for the repetition of his finished products. Machines did the work just as well and perhaps even better, and at a much smaller expense.

In the beginning of this industrial process man tried to meet it with aggressive action. But the nearer the avalanche of ghosts rolled towards him the more he tried other means of defense. He invented socialism and hoped that through changing the present state of production and distribution the mechanical device would become of even greater help and comfort to him than it had been.

One angle of the problem, however, has been overlooked. There is a way in which man, not through destructiveness nor through economic planning, but as a biological being and a creator, or as an association of creators, can fight back. It is through a strategy of creation which escapes the treachery of conservation and the competition of the robot. This strategy is the practice of the creative act, man, as a medium of creation, changing his products continuously. Spontaneity as a method of transition is as old as mankind, but as a focus in itself it is a problem of today and of tomorrow. If a fraction of one-thousandth of the energy which mankind has exerted in the conception and development of mechanical devices were to be used for the improvement of our cultural capacity during the moment of creation itself, mankind would enter into a new age of culture, a type of culture which would not have to dread any possible increase of machinery nor robot races of the future. The escape would be made without giving up anything that machine civilization has produced.

The eugenic doctrine, similarly to the technological process, is another promiser of extreme happiness to man. The eugenic dreamer sees in the distant future the human race so changed through breeding that all men will be born well, the world populated with heroes, saints, and Greek gods, and all that accomplished by certain techniques through the elimination and combination of genes. If this should really come to pass the world would be at once glorious, beautiful, and Godlike. But it may be reached at the cost of man as a creator from within himself; it would have, like Siegfried in the myth, a vulnerable spot into which the thorn of death could enter,—a tragic world, a world in which beauty, heroism, and wisdom are gained without effort, in which the hero is in want of the highest reward, the opportunity to rise from the humblest origin to a supreme level. It sums up to the question whether creation in its essence is finished with conception or whether creation does not continue or cannot be continued by the individual after he is born.

The eugenic dreamer and the technological dreamer have one idea in common: to substitute and hasten the slow process of nature. Once the creative process is encapsuled in a book it is given; it can be recapitulated eternally by everybody without the effort of creating anew. Once a machine for a certain pattern of performance is invented a certain product can be turned out in infinite numbers practically without the effort of man. Once that miraculous eugenic formula will be found a human society will be given at birth perfect and smooth, like a book off the press.

In the face of the two vehicles of thought and power, eugenic rule and machine rule, man ought to call to mind their meaning: that they both aim to remove the center and the rule from within him, the one into a process before he is conceived, the other into a process which is conserved, both aiming to make him uncreative. Technology may be able to improve the comfort of mankind and eugenics may be able to improve the health of mankind, but neither is able to decide what type of man can and should survive.

It is from the actual embodiment and performance of man within the psychological cross-currents which turn upon him from birth to death — that is, how he stands up in the psycho-geographical test, — that a decision, if any, can be made; and the conclusion we can draw from a survey of the position of man as a biological being in the world of today is that thrown into an industrial environment he does not stand up well in the conflict with the machine and that the solution of this conflict lies in an heroic measure, not to surrender to the machine, not to halt its development, but to meet it on even terms and to resort in this battle to resources which are inherent within his organism. Beyond the controversy, destruction of the unfit or survival of the fit, is a new goal, the survival of a flexible, spontaneous personality make-up, the survival of the creator.

• • • • • •

Herbert (Viscount) Samuel
Practical Ethics (1935)

During thousands of millions of years this earth has been in the making. Over a period of millions of years various forms of living beings have developed. Man slowly emerged many hundreds of thousands of years ago. Civilization has arisen within the last few thousands. Now we, of the living generation, take our place in the procession of the ages. But there is one difference between our times and all the times, remote or near, that have preceded. There is now, as never before, a race of beings on this planet which is aware of part at least of the cosmic process.

. . . . . .

[L]ittle by little, man has been building up the record of his own experience. He is now able, if he will, to draw the lessons. He may learn, if he will, how his civilization has grown—what has helped it and what has hindered. The development of language, of writing, of printing, has made possible the record itself, and its transmission from one generation to another. Libraries are the collective memory of mankind. We have at hand the materials for our own instruction.

There has always been evolution. Henceforth there may be Conscious Evolution.

. . . . . .

Ethics is an agent of conscious evolution, and an agent which plays a supremely important part. Reject or neglect the moral codes, whether personal or social or international, and the evolution of man into the future will on, as it must; but it will be towards a future not of continuous progress but of certain disaster.

. . . . . .

If conscious evolution is to be taken as the ruling principle, it is clearly essential that both philosophy and religion should do what science has done with such brilliant results, and escape from what has been called "the backward-looking habit." "No one can walk backwards into the future."

. . . . . .

We have grasped, in some degree, what is our own position as inheritors of the past and progenitors of the future. From now on, human evolution may become conscious. It need no longer be dependent on "senseless agencies." The change should greatly quicken the pace of progress—not only in things material, but in all things. And it should inspire a far greater confidence.

. . . . . .

Within the framework set by nature, the future evolution of mankind will depend upon the thoughts and the deeds of individual men and women, and upon nothing else. Each private act and each social activity, all the sciences and all the arts, take their place in one great scheme. It is for a wise philosophy to bring them into unison.

• • • • • •

Winston Churchill
"Mankind is Confronted by One Supreme Task" (1937)

Clearly, if things go on as they are, the human race is about to be subjected to processes of change more rapid and more fundamental than anything that has occurred in all history. In the next fifty years mankind will make greater progress in mastering and applying natural forces than in the last million years or more. That is a fearsome thought. And the first question we must ask ourselves is, 'Are we fit for it? Are we worthy of all these exalted responsibilities? Can we bear this tremendous strain?'

. . . . . .

The achievements of science in the nineteenth and twentieth centuries were not necessary to the happiness, virtue or glory of mankind. Endless possibilities of moral and mental improvement were open to us without any of the blessings or conveniences which we now enjoy. It is above all essential that man and woman of today should realize upon how much lower a plane science stands than that of manners and morals. It is far more important, for instance, to speak the truth oneself than to possess the most wonderful wireless set. It is much better to be kind and merciful than to whirl about in our fastest motorcars. It is far more splendid to keep one's word and be considerate toward other people than to be able to fly. Justice ranks far above steam. An upright, fearless judge renders a more exalted service than the cleverest inventor. Freedom is worth far more than electricity. The rights of the individual, a happy home and family, such as have existed even under hard, bleak conditions, are incomparably more precious than any amount of wonderful organization.

In so far as we can have both these sets of alternatives which I have contrasted, let us rejoice; but we shall fall indeed on evil days if we are forced to lose the old for the sake of the new. All this terrific material progress is really only valuable in so far as it liberates the innate goodness of the human heart. It would not be a blessing but a curse if it rolled forward uncontrolled by the moral principles of simple decent men and women. It can never be our salvation. It may be our doom.

. . . . . .

Are we the children of a glorious epoch advancing into the fullness of our inheritance, or are we simply a gang of squalid mischievous urchins who have got hold of firearms and raided the local laboratory for some tubes of typhus bacilli! Are we moving forward into a paradise of earthly delights where there will be enough for all, where the load of carking care about the means of existence—food, shelter, and clothing—will be lifted from the whole human race; or are we simply plunging into a senseless hell where all the treasures and joys of ordinary life will be calcined?

Broadly speaking, this is the supreme issue which now confronts us. We ought to think about it. Is it our power to decide? In my browner hours I sometimes doubt it. But then, one must always hope, for there is nothing so useless and so cowardly as despair. One must always try. It may not be in our power to decide the immediate future of the world, but it is our right and duty to choose – and to choose well.

• • • • • •

Hendrick van Loon
The Story of Mankind (1938)

THE IRON MAN

Originally the steam engine (like his younger brother, the
electric engine) had been a welcome addition to the family
of civilized human being because he was a willing slave and
ever ready to lighten the tasks of man and beast.

But soon it became clear that this inanimate factotum
was full of cunning and devilment and the war with its
temporary suspension of all the decencies of life gave the
iron contraption a chance to enslave those who in reality
were meant to be his masters.

Here and there some wise men of science may have
foreseen the danger that threatened the race from the side
of this unruly servant but as soon as such an unfortunate

prophet opened his mouth and issued a word of warning, he was denounced as an enemy of society, as a rank Bolshevik and a seditious radical and he was bade to hold his tongue or take the consequences. For the politicians and the diplomats who had been responsible for the war were now engaged upon the serious task of fabricating a suitable peace and they must not be interrupted in these holy endeavors. Unfortunately, as a class such worthies are almost always completely ignorant of those elementary principles of natural science and political economy which happen to dominate our present industrialized and mechanical form of society and they are less fit to handle complicated modern problems than any other group of men of whom I can think at the present moment. The plenipotentiaries of Paris [Treaty of Versailles] were no exception. They met in the shadow of the Iron Man, they talked of a world that was dominated by the Iron Man, yet never became aware of his presence and until the very end talked in words and symbols that represented the mentality of the eighteenth century but not that of the twentieth.

The result was inevitable. It is impossible to think in terms of the year 1719 and prosper in terms of the year 1919.

. . . . . .

I would say that [collapse] becomes unavoidable only when the cultural ideals of any given form of society no longer conform in any way to the actual conditions of life as people must live it in the pursuit of their daily affairs. You can watch that process in our own country. It is the nightmare of all our teachers who must initiate their pupils to one set of ideas, while life itself teaches them an entirely different one. It is the despair of our statesmen who feel that they are talking in a void. They preach one thing but their words will not carry weight until the actual facts of existence and the ideals according to which we strive to live shall once more have begun to be on speaking terms with each other and bear at least some vague resemblance to each other. During this intermediary period, while the old gods are dead and the new ones have not made their appearance, we must expect make-shift remedies, just as one expects a make-shift bridge when floods have washed away the old structure and the engineers are still working away at their blue-prints for the new one. If you look at the events in Germany and Russia and Japan and Italy and Spain and Turkey and almost everywhere else in the world, you suddenly begin to see them in a new light. Just for that, you won't like them any the better. But you will understand why they are as they happen to be and then you will have a lot more patience with them, for the leaders of these autocratic states are just as much the victims of the present social, economic and spiritual deluge as we ourselves.

And so there is nothing to do but make the best of a very uncomfortable bargain. We happened to have been born at the wrong moment, or at exactly the right moment, according to the way you happen to look at it. But those of us endowed with courage and the divine gift of curiosity have every reason to be contented. For it has been given unto us to be eye-witnesses of the most interesting spectacle ever shown on the stage of history and I for one am still enough of a believer in the ultimate fate of Man to accept these endless revulsions and convulsions of human society as the prologue to a new era, in which Mankind shall have at last the courage of its own convictions and shall boldly set forth to rid itself of its own worst enemy—its wilful ignorance and abysmal spiritual cowardice.

• • • • • •

J. Inglis Cameron
Letter to *The British Medical Journal* (1938)

In one respect...our circumstances are unique—we live in an age of "conscious" evolution. Each evolutionary step we take is not necessarily in the direction of progress; sometimes evolution leads us in a wrong direction. To-day, as soon as we realize that this has occurred, we have the power, if we will, of deliberately retrieving ourselves.

• • • • • •

To conclude the selections, we advance to 1959, to "The Evolutionary Vision"—the Darwin Centennial Convocation Address given by Sir Julian Huxley on the 100ᵗʰ anniversary of the publication of Darwin's On The Origin of Species. *Huxley was grandson of Thomas Huxley—one of the prominent evolutionary scholars of the 19ᵗʰ century—and brother of Aldous Huxley, author of* Brave New World. *"The Evolutionary Vision" was presented more than two decades after our last selection from the Industrial & Progressive Eras, but it recapitulates well some of the themes covered by the author's predecessors. It is also worth keeping in mind that this address was composed with World War II, the development of nuclear weapons, and the first decade of the Cold War in hindsight.*

Future historians will perhaps take this Centennial week as epitomizing an important critical period in the history of this earth of ours—the period when the process of evolution, in the person of inquiring man, began to be truly conscious of itself.

· · · · · ·

In 1859, Darwin opened the passage leading to a new psychosocial level, with a new pattern of ideological organization—an evolution-centered organization of thought and belief...To those who did not deliberately shut their eyes or who were not allowed to look, it was at once clear that the fact and concept of evolution was bound to act as the central germ or living template of a new dominant thought organization. And in the century since the *Origin of Species*, there have been many attempts to understand the implications of evolution in many fields, from the affairs of the stellar universe to the affairs of men, and to integrate the facts of evolution and our knowledge of its processes into the over-all organization of our general thought.

. . . . . .

[Man] has been ousted from his self-imagined centrality in the universe to an infinitesimal location in a peripheral position in one of a million of galaxies. Nor, it would appear, is he likely to be unique as a sentient being. On the other hand, the evolution of mind or sentiency is an extremely rare event in the vast meaninglessness of the insentient universe, and man's particular brand of sentiency may well be unique. But in any case he is highly significant. He is a reminder of the existence, here and there, in the quantitative vastness of cosmic matter and its energy equivalents, of a trend toward mind, with its accompaniment of quality and richness of existence—and, what is more, a proof of the importance of mind and quality in the all-embracing evolutionary process.

It is only through possessing a mind that he has become the dominant portion of this planet and the agent responsible for its future evolution; and it will be only by the right use of that mind that he will be able to exercise that responsibility rightly. He could all too readily be a failure in the job; he will succeed only if he faces it consciously and if he uses all his mental resources—of knowledge and reason, of imagination, sensitivity, and moral effort.

And he must face it unaided by outside help. In the evolutionary pattern of thought there is no longer either need or room for the supernatural.

. . . . . .

We have only recently emerged from the biological to the psychosocial area of evolution, from the earthy biosphere into the freedom of the noosphere...Our feet still drag in the biological mud, even when we lift our heads into the conscious air. But, unlike those remote ancestors of ours, we can truly see something of the promised land beyond. We can do so with the aid of our new instrument of vision—our rational, knowledge-based imagination. Like the earliest pre-Galilean telescopes, it is still a very primitive instrument and gives a feeble and often distorted view. But, like the early telescopes, it is capable of immense improvement and could reveal many secrets of our noospheric home and destiny.

Meanwhile, no mental telescope is required to see the immediate evolutionary landscape and the frightening problems which inhabit it. All that is needed—but that is plenty!—is for us to cease being intellectual and moral ostriches and take our heads out of the sand of wilful blindness. If we do so, we shall soon see that the alarming problems are two-faced and are also stimulating challenges.

What are those alarming monsters in our evolutionary path? I would list them as follows. The threat of superscientific war, nuclear, chemical, and biological; the threat of overpopulation; the rise and appeal of Communist ideology, especially in the underprivileged sectors of the world's people; the failure to bring China, with nearly a quarter of the world's population, into the world organization of the United Nations; the erosion of the world's cultural variety; our general preoccupation with means rather than ends, with technology and quantity rather than creativity and quality; and the revolution of expectation caused by the widening gap between the haves and the have-nots, between the rich and the poor nations.

. . . . . .

We attempt to deal with these problems piecemeal, often halfheartedly...In reality, they are not separate monsters, to be dealt with by a series of separate ventures, however heroic or saintly. They are all symptoms of a new evolutionary situation; and this can be successfully met only in the light and with the aid of a new organization of thought and belief, a new dominant pattern of ideas.

It is hard to break through the firm framework of an accepted belief system and build a new acceptable successor, but it is necessary. It is necessary to organize our ad hoc ideas and scattered values into a unitive pattern, transcending conflicts and divisions in its unitary web. Only by such a reconciliation of opposites and disparates can our belief-system release us from inner conflicts; only so can we gain that peaceful assurance that will help unlock our energies for development in strenuous practical action.

Somehow or other, we must make our new pattern of thinking evolution-centered.

. . . . . .

Our new organization of thought—belief-system, framework of values, ideology, call it what you will— must grow and be developed in the light of our new evolutionary vision. So, in the first place, it must, of course, itself be evolutionary. That is to say, it must help us to think in terms of an overriding process of change, development, and possible improvement; to have our eyes on the future rather than on the past; to find support in the growing body of our knowledge, not in fixed dogma or ancient authority.

. . . . . .

The individual need not feel just a meaningless cog in the social machine or merely the helpless prey and sport of vast impersonal forces. He can do something to develop his own personality, to develop his own talents and possibilities, to interact personally and fruitfully with other individuals. If so, in his own person, he is effecting an important realization of evolutionary possibility; he is contributing his own personal quality to the fulfilment of human destiny. He has assurance of his own significance in the greater and more enduring whole of which he is part.

• • • • • •

Afterword

Huxley interacted in the 1950s with a new generation of thinkers, including some of the founders of modern systems theory who would continue to build on the "New Sciences" of the earlier generation and seek to apply them to the world's challenges. A branch of that field of inquiry became known as Evolutionary Systems Theory (or General Evolutionary Theory)—what I see as the most direct continuation of the earlier heritage dating to the mid-1800s. Some of the prominent thinkers emerging in this field in the 1970s include Erich Jantsch, Ervin Laszlo, and Jonas Salk.

In the 1980s, several of these individuals, joined by others from a wide range of disciplines—from social science to biology to astrophysics—formed a General Evolution Research Group that remained active for some years. A notable branching of thought among members of this group, as reported to me, was between those whose interest was primarily theoretical and those with more of a focus on action to improve the human condition.

Today I have a difficult time identifying "general evolutionary" thought and writing that possesses the originality, insight, and power of the expressions of earlier generations. This may reflect my own bias. But perhaps the foundation had indeed been laid long ago, and it is up to current and future generations to bridge theory with action. I think that new generations would be inspired, informed, and empowered by the larger story—what some have called the evolutionary epic—and by the knowledge of the modern roots of evolutionary consciousness.

The Journey Continues

It is my hope that through this anthology the reader has, at the very least, gained new insight into a new pattern of thinking that was evident in a time of tremendous change in human society. I also hope that the reader can draw some inspiration from that time—perhaps something that tells them that they have not been alone in seeing, or at least sensing, a bigger story at play. That bigger story is about a fresh unfolding of the process of evolution, of which we are a part. But the reader would not be alone in asking "what happened?"—e.g., given that the Industrial and Progressive Eras saw such a flowering of evolutionary awareness, and the beginnings of conscious evolution, why are we still in such a mess more than a century later?

It is my interpretation that the transition from unconscious evolution to conscious evolution that was sparked in the mid-1800s has continued to unfold. However, it did not appear to take root broadly in its first wave. In the wake of the intellectual revolutions, new sciences, and change movements seen in the early part of the 20th century, the industrial worldview prevailed, education became stuck in form, and ostensibly democratic politics became the domain of professionals and parties. Patterns characteristic of the era of unconscious evolution were carried forward into the 20th century, and then into our 21st. In the interim between the time period surveyed and today, we experienced another world war even more devastating and disconcerting than the first; the development of nuclear weapons and the associated specter of the Cold War; a wealth gap continuing to expand through today; political polarization and anti-democratic forms of populism; worldwide loss of habitats and species, and the increasingly visible effects of an accelerating and disastrous climate change attributed at least in part to human activity, which we seem unwilling to collectively address.

Setbacks, disappointments, and new challenges notwithstanding, the overall movement toward progressive liberation and integration never stopped. From the 1960s onward, we saw the maturing of environmental awareness, anti-war movements, significant advances in racial and gender equality and equity, the sunset of colonialism (at least the classical version of it), the end of the Cold War, and an information revolution that opened up new possibilities for billions of people. War still exists, although we may be grateful that for the most part, the trend of its deadliness has been steeply downward.

The deeper tide of evolutionary transformation continues to rise. There is a palpable tension between the expectation of *better* for *more* and the collective inertia hindering us from making it so. Tensions between the old and new patterns continue to grow while change continues to accelerate. So do reactions against that change. There are a lot of people doing good things—for justice, for human development, for protection of the living systems of the earth—and in far more ways than could be found in the late 1800s and early 1900s. Yet relatively few people see or experience *evolutionary agency*, which comes from the combination of evolutionary awareness and conscious efforts to shift away from the fundamental patterns in culture and society that keep creating problems toward those that help us understand, prevent, and solve them.

We have a long way to go in the maturation toward a global capacity for conscious evolution—specifically the conscious evolution of culture and society, in a participatory manner, toward greater support for human development and a thrivable relationship with the natural environment on which we all depend. Yet I hope that we can draw faith from the story told through this anthology, and in taking stock of the quality and quantity of positive change that has occurred within just our own lifetimes, that there may be an *inevitability* to this shift. Whether or not the continuation of the grand evolutionary journey on earth—through this shift into conscious evolution—is inevitable, it seems that we must work to make it happen. What forms can that work take? One form—what we might call evolutionary *witnessing*—is represented by this collection of writings. It tends to come out of the academic world but some are making efforts to build bridges to a general audience. I also believe that there is a great need for *evolutionary advocacy and activism* at the local level. By this I mean educational and political work to build capacities for shifting culture out of the old and unconscious patterns and into new, conscious ones appropriate for our times.

For the reader who undertakes the challenge of helping move us toward conscious evolution, I wish you courage, creativity, vision, support, and success.

Sources

"A Misconception of History." Editorial. *The Spectator*, No. 2, 928, August 9, 1884.

Ashcroft, Edgar A. *The World's Desires*. Kegan Paul, Trench, Trubner & Co., 1905.

Beck, J.M. Comments about Edward Dean Adams upon Adams' award of the John Fritz Medal. *Journal of the American Institute of Electrical Engineers* Vol. XLV, No. 5, May 1926.

Bennett, Jesse Lee, ed. *The American Tradition*. George H. Doran Co., 1925.

Bernard, L.L. "The Conditions of Social Progress." *The American Journal of Sociology*, Vol. 28, No. 1, July 1922.

Bernard, L.L. "Invention and Social Progress." *The American Journal of Sociology*, Vol. 29, No. 3, July 1923.

Bixby, James Thompson. *The Ethics of Evolution* (2nd edition). American Unitarian Association, 1907.

Bobbitt, Franklin. *The Curriculum*. Houghton, Mifflin, 1918.

Boodin, John Elof. *Cosmic Evolution: Outlines of Cosmic Idealism*. The Macmillan Company, 1925.

Branford, Benchara. *A New Chapter in the Science of Government*. Chatto & Windus, 1919.

Brosius, Mariott. "The Medical Profession and the State." Graduation oration, Medico-Chirurgical College of Philadelphia. *The Medical Bulletin*, Vol. XVII, No. 6, June 1895.

Burroughs, E.A., Bishop of Ripon. Address to members of the British Association for the Advancement of Science in Leeds,

September 4, 1927, as reported in *The New York Times*, September 5, 1927.

Bushnell, Charles J. "The Place of Religion in Modern Life." *American Journal of Theology*, Vol. XVII, No. 4, October 1913.

Cairnes, J.E. "Social Evolution." *Popular Science Monthly*, Vol. 6, March 1875.

Cameron, J. Inglis. Letter to *Supplement to The British Medical Journal*, February 26, 1938.

Catt, Carrie Chapman. "Evolution and Woman's Suffrage." Speech before the National American Woman Suffrage Association at the Congress of Representative Women, Chicago, May 18, 1893.

Catt, Carrie Chapman. "A Christmas Greeting to the New Woman Voters." *Ourselves*, Vol. 11, No 12, December 1919.

Catt, Carrie Chapman. "Evolution—Fifty Years Ago: A Reminiscence." *The Woman Citizen*, Vol. X, No. 4, July 11, 1925.

Churchill, Winston. "Mankind is Confronted by One Supreme Task." *News of the World*, November 14, 1937.

Clapperton, Jane Hume. *Scientific Meliorism and the Evolution of Happiness*. London: Kegan Paul, Trench & Co., 1885.

Cohen, Chapman. *A Grammar of Freethought*. The Pioneer Press, 1921.

Conklin, Edwin Grant. "Has Progressive Evolution Come to an End?" *Natural History*, Vol. 19, No. 1, January 1919.

Conklin, Edwin Grant. *The Direction of Human Evolution*. Charles Scribner's Sons, 1921.

Conn, Herbert William. *Social Heredity and Social Evolution: The Other Side of Eugenics.* The Abington Press, 1914.

Cooley, Charles Horton. *Social Organization.* Charles Scribner's Sons, 1909.

Dabney, Charles W., Jr., Commencement speech. Virginia Polytechnic Institute, 1896.

Darsie, Marvin L. "The Spiritual in Education." *Los Angeles School Journal*, Vol. 8, No. 5, October 3, 1924.

Davidson, Thomas. *A History of Education.* Charles Scribner's Sons, 1907.

Davis, Robert Gunn. "Some Tendencies in Social Evolution." *Westminster Review*, Vol. CLXIX, No. 1, January 1908.

de Bothezat, George. "The Meaning for Humanity of the Aerial Crossing of the Ocean." *The Scientific Monthly*, Vol. 9, No. 5, November 1919.

Dewey, John. "Democracy in Education." *The Elementary School Teacher*, Vol. IV, No. 4, December 1903.

Dyer, Henry. *Evolution of Industry.* New York: Macmillan & Co., 1895.

Ecob, James Henry. "Studies in Social Christianity: Interdependence." *The Homiletic Review*, Vol. LXIX, No.5, May 1915.

Ellis, William. *Thoughts on the Future of The Human Race.* London: Smith, Elder & Co., 1866.

Ellwood, Charles A. *The Psychology of Human Society.* D. Appleton & Company, 1925.

Ellwood, Charles A. *Cultural Evolution*. The Century Co., 1927.

Ely, Richard T. *Studies in the Evolution of Industrial Society*. The Macmillan Co., 1903.

"Evolutionary Agencies." *The Arbitrator*, Vol. III, No. 7, December 1920.

Faris, Ellsworth. "The Nature of Human Nature." *Papers and Proceedings of the Twentieth Annual Meeting, December 1925, American Sociological Society*, Vol. XX, July 1926,

Floyd, William (Ed.) Dedication. *Social Progress: A Handbook of the Liberal Movement*. The Arbitrator, 1925.

Follett, Mary Parker. *The New State*. Longmans, Green, 1918.

Geddes, Patrick. *Cities in Evolution*. Williams & Norgate, 1915.

Geddes, Patrick. *Ideas at War*. Williams & Norgate, 1917.

Goode, J. Paul. "The Human Response to the Physical Environment." *The Elementary School Teacher*, Vol. 4, No. 5, January 1904.

Gray, L.C. "The Economic Possibilities of Conservation." *The Quarterly Journal of Economics*, Vol. 27, No. 3, May 1913.

Greenlaw, Asbury Lincoln. *Resident Forces of Life, The Evolution of Humanity*. Plymouth Publishing Company, 1917.

Harrison, Frederic. "A Few Words About the Nineteenth Century." *The Fortnightly Review*, Vol. XXXI, No. CLXXXI, April 1, 1882.

Hart, Joseph K. *The Discovery of Intelligence*. The Century Co., 1924.

Herrick, Judson. *Neurological Foundations of Animal Behavior.* Henry Holt & Co., 1924.

Hertzler, J.O. "Social Immortality." *Prairie Schooner*, Vol. II, No.2, Spring 1928.

Hird, Dennis. *An Easy Outline of Evolution.* Watts & Co., 1903.

Hobhouse, L.T., *Mind in Evolution* (1st Edition). MacMillan Co., 1901.

Howerth, Ira W. "Education and Social Progress." *Educational Review*, Vol. XXIII, No. 4, April 1902.

Howerth, Ira W. "The Social Ideal." *International Journal of Ethics*, Vol. 18, No. 2, January 1908.

Huxley, Julian. "The Evolutionary Vision" (1959). In Tax & Callender, Eds., *Evolution After Darwin, Vol. 3: Issues in Evolution*, University of Chicago Press, 1960.

Janes, Lewis G. "Cosmic Evolution, as Related to Ethics." In *Life and the Conditions of Survival: The Physical Basis of Ethics, Sociology and Religion – Popular Lectures and Discussions Before the Brooklyn Ethical Association.* Chicago: Charles H. Kerr & Co.,1895.

Jones, Henry. "Social and Individual Evolution." *The New World*, No. XXVII, September 1898. Reprinted in Jones, Henry, *The Working Faith of the Social Reformer and Other Essays*, MacMillan and Co., 1910.

Jones, William Carey, "The Conditions of a Californian Civilization." *The University Chronicle*, Volume II, University of California at Berkeley, 1899.

Kamiat, Arnold H. "The Basis of Society." *Philosophy*, Vol. 9, No. 33, January 1934.

Kelloway, Warwick Freeman. *The Ethics of Achievement.* 1925. McGill University, Master's Thesis.

Kidd, Benjamin. *Principles of Western Civilisation.* Macmillan and Co., 1902.

Kilpatrick, William H. "The Demand of the Times Upon Our Schools." *Teachers College Record,* Vol. XXII, No. 2, March 1921.

Kilpatrick, William H. *Education for a Changing Civilization.* MacMillan, 1926.

Kimball, John C. *The Romance of Evolution and its Relation to Religion.* American Unitarian Association, 1913.

Kracht, George V. "Social Ideals and Social Progress." *International Journal of Ethics,* Vol. 27, No. 4, July 1917.

Le Conte, Joseph. "The Factors of Evolution," *The Monist,* Vol. 1, No. 3, April 1891.

Leppington, Blanche. "The Debrutalization of Man." *Eclectic Magazine of Foreign Literature, Science, and Art,* Vol. LXII, No. 2, August 1895.

Lowell, Edward J. Letter in response to "A Misconception of History." *The Spectator,* No. 2, 932, September 6, 1884.

Loy, Mina. "Psycho-Democracy" (pamphlet). Reproduced in *The Little Review: A Quarterly Journal of Arts and Letters,* August 1921.

Macdonald, Carolyn. "Woman Suffrage and Evolution." (Letter to the Editor). *The Forum,* Vol. LXXII, No. 4, October 1924.

Maeterlinck, Maurice. *The Measure of the Hours.* Dodd, Mead, & Co., 1907.

Marsh, George P. *Man and Nature.* New York: Charles Scribner & Co., 1864, 1867.

Marsh, George P. *The Earth as Modified by Human Action.* New York: Scriber, Armstrong & Co.,1874.

Marvin, F.S. "Science and Human Affairs," in *Science and Civilization*, F.S. Marvin, Ed. Oxford University Press, 1923.

McCabe, Joseph. *Can We Save Civilisation?* The Search Publishing Co., 1932.

McCabe, Joseph. *The A B C of Evolution.* G.P. Putnam's Sons, 1920.

McGilvary, Evander Bradley. "The Warfare of Moral Ideals." *Hibbert Journal*, Vol. XIV, No. 1, 1916.

Mecklin, John M. *An Introduction to Social Ethics: The Social Conscience in a Democracy.* Harcourt, Brace and Howe, 1922.

Meredith, William John. *The Evolution of Democracy.* The People's Institute, 1916.

Millikan, Robert A. "Science and Modern Life." The Atlantic Monthly, Vol. 141, No. 4, April 1928.

Montague, Francis C. *The Limits of Individual Liberty: An Essay.* London: Rivingtons, 1885.

Moreno, J.L. *Who Shall Survive?* Nervous and Mental Disease Publishing Co., 1934.

Mukerjee, Radhakamal. "Borderlands of Economics." *Indian Journal of Economics*, Vol. V, Part 2, 1925.

Mukerjee, Radhakamal. "The Ecological Outlook in Sociology." *The American Journal of Sociology*, Vol. 35, No. 3, November 1932.

Newton, Joseph Fort. "Salvation by Education." Baccalaureate Address, University of Virginia, 1922.

Noble, Edmund. *Purposive Evolution*. Henry Holt and Company, 1926.

Ogburn, William F. *Social Change with Respect to Culture and Original Nature*. B.W. Huebsch, 1922.

Ogburn, William F, and Gilfillan, Seabury C. "The Influence of Invention and Discovery." *US President's Research Committee on Social Trends, Recent Social Trends in the United States*, Volume 1. McGraw-Hill, 1933.

Partridge, G.E. *The Psychology of Nations*. The Macmillan Co., 1919.

Patten, William. *The Grand Strategy of Evolution: The Social Philosophy of a Biologist*. Richard G. Badger, 1920.

Perry-Coste, F.H. (a.k.a. A Free Lance). *Towards Utopia: Being Speculations in Social Evolution*. New York: D. Appleton and Co., 1894.

Pickens, William. *The New Negro*. The Neale Publishing Company, 1916.

Powell, E.P., *Our Heredity from God*. D. Appleton & Co., 1887.

Prince, Morton. "A World Consciousness and Future Peace." Address before the Concordia Association of Japan, June 13, 1916, Tokyo. *The Journal of Abnormal Psychology*, Vol. XI, 1916.

Quarterly Newsbook of the Municipal University. Kansas City: Municipal University Press, 1907.

Ravenhill, Alice. Quoted in Ellen H. Richards, *Euthenics: The Science of Controllable Environment*. Whitcomb & Barrows, 1910.

Reclus, Elisée. "The Progress of Mankind." *The Contemporary Review*, Vol. LXX, December 1896.

Reade, (William) Winwood. *The Martyrdom of Man*. London: Trubner & Co., 1872.

Reid, Archdall. "Characters, Congenital and Acquired." *Science*, Vol. 6, No. 156, Dec. 24, 1897.

Richard, Ernst. *God's Path to Peace: A Story of Evolution*. The Abdington Press, 1914.

Robinson, James Harvey. "The New History." *Proceedings of the American Philosophical Society*, Vol. 50, No. 199, May-August 1911.

Robinson, James Harvey. *The New History: Essays Illustrating the Modern Historical Outlook*. Macmillan, 1912.

Rust, Francis Marion. *The Evolution of Democracy*. Printing press of Armenian diocese of Azerbaijan, 1923.

Samuel, Herbert (Viscount). *Practical Ethics*. Oxford University Press, 1935.

Sarton, George. "The New Humanism." *Isis*, 1924.

Savage, Minot J. "The Effects of Evolution on The Coming Civilization." Lecture before the Brooklyn Ethical Association. The New Ideal Publishing Co., 1889.

Seashore, Carl Emil. Speech before the Annual Meeting of the American Peace Society, Washington, DC, May 26, 1922.

Seth, James. "The Evolution of Morality." *Mind*, Vol. 14, No. 53, January 1889.

Small, Albion W. and George E. Vincent. *An Introduction to the Study of Society*. New York: American Book Company, 1894.

Spence, Catherine Helen. "A Week in the Future." Serialized in *The Centennial Magazine*. Sydney: December 1888-July 1889.

Spencer, Herbert. *Principles of Sociology*. London: Williams and Norgate, 1874.

Spiller, Gustav. "The Interpretation of Sociological Data." *The American Journal of Sociology*, Vol. 21, No. 4, January 1916.

Sprague, Leslie Willis. "The Ethical Reorganization of the Social Ideal." Lecture before the Brooklyn Society for Ethical Culture. In *Ethical Addresses and Ethical Record*, Sixteenth Series, The American Ethical Union, 1909.

Staars, David. *The English Woman: Studies in Her Psychic Evolution*. Smith, Elder & Co., 1909.

Strong, Rev. Josiah. *The New Era or The Coming Kingdom*. New York: The Baker & Taylor Co., 1893.

Swift, Morrison I. Massachusetts, House. House Bill No. 1247. Changing the Prisons into Social Schools (Bill accompanying petition of Morrison L. Swift), January 17, 1912.

Swift, Morrison I. *Can Mankind Survive*. Marshall Jones Co., 1919.

Taft, Jessie. *The Woman Movement from the Point of View of Social Consciousness*. The Collegiate Press, 1915.

Tayler, J. Lionel. "Aspects of Individual Evolution." *The Westminster Review*, Vol. CLXV, No. 6, June 1906.

Teilhard de Chardin, Fr. Pierre. "A Note on Progress." Essay dated 1920, unpublished until appearance in *The Future of Man*, Éditions du Seuil, 1959; English translation Harper & Row, 1964.

Thomson, J. Arthur. *What is Man*. G.P. Putnam's Sons, 1924.

Tuttle, Florence Guertin. *The Awakening of Woman: Suggestions from the Psychic Side of Feminism*. The Abdington Press, 1915.

Tylor, Edward B. "Primitive Society." *The Contemporary Review*, Vol. 22, June 1873.

Untermann, Ernest. *Science and Revolution*. Charles H. Kerr & Co., 1905.

Van Loon, Hendrick. *The Story of Mankind*. Boni & Liveright, 1921.

Van Loon, Hendrick. *The Story of Mankind*. Garden City Publishing Co., 1938.

Vestal, C.L. "The Meaning of American Democracy." *The Standard*, Vol. III, No. 4, January 1917.

Wallas, Graham. *The Great Society*. Macmillan and Co., 1914.

Weiss, Albert P. "The Aims of Social Evolution." *The Ohio Journal of Science*, Vol. 23, No. 3, May-June 1923.

Welch, John S. *Literature in the School*. Silver, Burdett & Co., 1910.

Wells, H.G. "An Apology for a World Utopia." In F.S. Marvin (ed.), *The Evolution of World Peace*. Oxford University Press, 1921.

Wells, H.G. *The Open Conspiracy: Blue Prints for a World Revolution*. Victor Gollancz Ltd., 1928/1933.

Weyl, Walter E. *The New Democracy*, Revised Edition. The Macmillan Company, 1914.

Whitehead, Alfred North. *Science and the Modern World*. MacMillan, 1925.

Whitehead, Alfred North. *Adventures of Ideas*. Macmillan, 1933.

Wilkin, George F., *Control in Evolution*. A.C. Armstrong & Son, 1903.

Wilshire, Gaylord. *Wilshire Editorials*. Wilshire Book Co., 1906.

Wissler, Clark. *Man and Culture*. Thomas Y. Crowell Co., 1923.

Yard, Robert Sterling. "The Place of Our National Parks in Education." *Bulletin of the National Parks Association*, October 9, 1923.

About the Editor

Matthew Shapiro is an independent researcher, writer, and community organizer with a longstanding interest in our collective capacity for dialogue, participatory democracy, and the participatory design of social systems. He has more than three decades of experience in working to bridge theories of participatory democracy and design with practice at the neighborhood level and in the arenas of education, community engagement, and local governance. This work drew the attention and support of leading thinkers, including virologist Jonas Salk, psychologist Mihaly Csikszentmihalyi, and participatory design pioneer Bela H. Banathy.

A former teacher, he founded an innovative community-based charter school, where he taught the middle school group. He then went through the doctoral program in Curriculum and Instruction at Boise State University, where his focus was on the barriers to systemic change in education.

Published works include numerous critical research reports, workbooks to assist in public participation in educational design, and articles and book chapters spanning the social sciences. These include articles in *The Eastern Anthropologist* and *World Futures: The Journal of General Evolution*, and invited chapters in *Dialogue as a Means of Collective Communication* and other books.

A native of Brooklyn, New York, he has called Boise, Idaho home for the past thirty years.